ELIOT'S
FOUR QUARTETS

By the same author

Novels
The Good Pit Man
The Lover Next Door
The Rector's Daughter

Criticism
The Making of George Orwell:
An Essay in Literary History

The Visual Imagination of D. H. Lawrence

Eliot's
Four Quartets

Poetry as Chamber Music

Keith Alldritt

THE WOBURN PRESS

First published 1978 in Great Britain by
THE WOBURN PRESS
Gainsborough House, Gainsborough Road,
London E11 1RS, England

and in the United States of America by
THE WOBURN PRESS
c/o Biblio Distribution Centre
81 Adams Drive, P.O. Box 327, Totowa, N.J. 07511

British Library Cataloguing in Publication Data

Alldrit, Keith
    Eliot's 'Four quartets'.
    1. Eliot, Thomas Stearns, Four quartets
    I. Title
    821'.9'12   PS3509.L43F6

    ISBN 0–7130–0161–5

Printed in Great Britain by The Bourne Press, Bournemouth

For

Philip and Ruth Pinkus

The reduction in volume of sound and the renouncing of broader effects in chamber music make it possible to organise the structure right through to its innermost cells and differentials . . . . . Even in Beethoven's last quartets the refusal of monumentality permits an inner structure operating at every single moment such as would have been incompatible with the *al fresco* manner of the symphony. Such composing was encouraged by the essential medium of chamber music, the individual voices which emerge independently yet continually condition each other. As a reaction against the expansive and the decorative, the medium was essentially critical, 'about things' and in late Beethoven, anti-ideological . . . While chamber music is less concerned than symphony to establish an external solidarity — the illusionary solidarity of the auditors — it is also, due to its richly and finely woven net of thematic relationships, more unified and integral. It is also, because of its more fully realised individualisations, freer, more autonomous, less violent. The apparent loss of thematic extensiveness in the recourse to private experience is compensated for by its secessional, windowless compellingness.

Theodor W. Adorno

Contents

Preface

Though the status of T. S. Eliot's *Four Quartets* as a major, if not *the* major poem in British literature of this century is generally allowed, the particular qualities and achievement of the work remain only very partially investigated. The poem has elicited, to be sure, some fine pieces of explication, analysis and evaluation. But the critical discussion as a whole still has far to go before it will start to do justice to the range, the intricacy and the ambitiousness of the work. The sequence is, as Eliot himself is reported to have said, his principal work.[1] Yet the critical attention which the poem has received has never been as active, as continuous or as voluminous as that devoted to *The Waste Land*. The essays that follow are intended to help to repair this deficiency in the response to a major literary work and to re-assess its importance in the history of modern poetry.

My purpose is not just to describe certain features of the poem but to relate it to a tradition of poetic theory and practice which originated more than a century ago and which still continues strong well over thirty years after *Four Quartets* was completed. A principal characteristic of this tradition is the employment of a set of analogies between poetry and music in order to regenerate the art of poetry and its medium of language. (The two most considerable English poems of the 1960s, Basil Bunting's 'sonata' *Briggflatts* and Roy Fisher's *The Ship's*

11

Orchestra perpetuate very explicitly this tradition of analogy.)
Each of the three essays that follow deals with an aspect of
this principle of musicality as it informs *Four Quartets*. The
well established, theoretical metaphor of music is but a perspective, a device for talking very particularly about certain
qualities of words and of methods of employing them. The
words of the poem are my chief concern. For in my view the
achievement represented by the work is pre-eminently verbal.
This special quality is far more important than any issues of
philosophy, theology or mysticism to which the work alludes
and which sometimes divert readers from the assessment of
the poem as a poem into agreement or disagreement with it
as an ideological statement. *Four Quartets* is a poem, a poem
that struggles to employ the fullest powers of the medium of
English as these were available during the thirties and forties
of this century. And it is a poem that can be seen to belong
to a tradition of similarly strenuous, subtle, patiently careful
workings with language. This essential quality of *Four Quartets*
is the main subject of this book. The poem refers intermittently
to matters of thought, philosophy and belief but its full nature,
meaning and value can only be approached by assuming it
as a poem, a thing of words.

In trying to formulate my own understanding of the un-
ending resonances and the multiplicity of verbal methods of
the poem, I have been greatly helped by those who have
preceded me in writing about *Four Quartets*. I am especially
indebted to the work of Helen Gardner, Raymond Preston,
Donald Davie, Hugh Kenner and Harry Blamires. I should
also like to thank those who have assisted in the actual writing
of this book. Joan Hardwick typed the manuscript and
collaborated with me in every stage of its revision and improvement. To the Canada Council I am indebted for a leave
fellowship which gave me time to complete the work.

12

Introduction

Introduction

In the last of the quartets Eliot relates the experience of a strange dawn meeting in London after an air raid. The ghostly figure whom he encounters is a composite of all his dead masters in the art of poetry. The identities of some of these teachers may be readily deduced from the many allusions in this passage and in others elsewhere in the sequence. But the presence of Mallarmé in this company is established emphatically and unmistakeably by the direct citation of an important line from one of his poems. In his sonnet of homage to one of his own dead masters, Edgar Allan Poe, Mallarmé defines a function of poetry in a striking line that recurs in almost word for word translation in the speech of the dawn figure who addresses Eliot. The sixth line of Mallarmé's sonnet 'Le Tombeau d'Edgar Poe' describes the poetic enterprise as 'Donner un sens plus pur aux mots de la tribu'. The phrase is repeated in the second line of this sentence spoken by Eliot's teacher:

Since our concern was speech, and speech impelled us
   To purify the dialect of the tribe
   And urge the mind to aftersight and foresight,

Let me disclose the gifts reserved for age
To set a crown upon your lifetime's effort.

The idea of what these crowning gifts are is also common to both passages. Put simply, the suggestion is that the poet, like anyone else, will undergo suffering and death but that the poem, if it is a purified, refined act of language, may continue to be inasmuch as it continues as a part of the verbal consciousness of those who live after. This notion of the special functions of pure language and pure poetry so prominent in Mallarmé's thinking proves to be an important reference (though not a shared assumption) in Eliot's poem.

Such explicit references to the work of Mallarmé in 'Little Gidding' (there are others elsewhere in *Four Quartets*) are part of a concern with the theory and practice of the French symbolist poets that can be seen to continue throughout Eliot's career. In a lecture on the symbolists given when he was sixty, Eliot stated 'I recognise first that within this tradition from Poe to Valéry are some of those modern poems which I most admire and enjoy; second I think that the tradition itself represents the most interesting development of poetic consciousness anywhere in that same hundred years . . . .'[2] Hugh Kenner offers the following summary of the effects of this admiration upon Eliot's development as a poet: 'Eliot after some years' infatuation with a peripheral Symbolist poet, Jules Laforgue, worked more and more deeply into the central Symbolist poetic, translated Perse, sponsored the reputation of Valéry in England, and wrote his last principal work, the *Four Quartets,* under the sign of Mallarmé himself and with a title that remembers Verlaine ("De la musique avant toute chose").'[3]

In the three essays that follow I shall consider *Four Quartets*

16

as a symbolist poem and try to assess the extent to which its procedures, meaning and value may be illuminated by relating them to some of the principal ideas in the symbolist poetic. At the same time, through detailed attention to this one important poem, I want to attempt some further description of the symbolist tradition itself. *Four Quartets* can be seen to constitute a distinctive stage in the long development of this tradition. The phases of a certain kind of poetic activity that are signified by the names, Baudelaire, Verlaine, Rimbaud, Mallarmé, and then outside France by Blok, George, Yeats and Eliot continue into more recent years. There are, for instance, significant references to Mallarmé in the work of Louis Zukofsky, of Basil Bunting and of Roy Fisher. The methods of *Four Quartets* refer back to seventy years of difficult poetic endeavour; they also point forward to, and help to explain the concerns and endeavours of the important poetry of the present time. Each of the essays that follows treats a particular characteristic of this tradition. In these introductory paragraphs I shall try to establish certain rudimentary facts about the history of symbolist practice and theory during the last hundred and twenty years or so.

Poems from the later phase of symbolism are often difficult and abstruse. But the first impulse behind recognisably symbolist activity was not at all problematical. It was simply an insistence upon the need for a respect for the medium of language. ' . . . Baudelaire was not a disciple of Swinburne: for Baudelaire every word counts,' wrote Eliot in the essay 'Baudelaire In Our Time' in which he reviews some translations from Baudelaire by Arthur Symons. He goes on to define a chief failing in Symons's work as 'an impotence to use words definitely, to use words at all unless they are the few poor counters of habitual and lazy sentiment'.[4] A careful,

17

respectful attention to the word, a scrupulous concern to employ it properly is the initial and continuing emphasis of the symbolist tradition. The rich resonance of individual words is one of the more immediately striking features of *Four Quartets* and this same quality continues to be present in *Briggflatts* just as it had been in *Les Fleurs du Mal*. Baudelaire himself tells us something of the origins of this concern. In his essay on Gautier who so compelled his (and later Mallarmé's) admiration, Baudelaire recalls how this issue was raised at their very first meeting and became an important assumption in the friendship that developed between them:

> He then asked me, with a curiously suspicious eye, and as though to put me to the test, if I liked reading dictionaries. The question was put with the calm manner he brings to all he says, and in a tone of voice someone else might have adopted to inquire whether I preferred reading travel books or fiction. Fortunately, I had been seized very young with lexicomania, and I saw that my stock had risen as a result of my reply.[5]

The programme of close attention to the individual word and also to the other basic units of poetry, the line, the phrase and the sentence was established far earlier in France than in England. Gautier's repudiation of the verbal casualness and looseness of romantic poets such as Lamartine, de Musset and Hugo first occurred in the 1830s. No such doctrine of concern for the particulars of language was drawn up in the English speaking world until the formation of the principles of imagism by Pound and his associates in 1912.

Gautier's prescriptions for the writing of poetry are to be

found in some well known lines in his poem 'L'Art' in the volume *Emaux et Camées*:

> Point de contraintes fausses!
> Mais que pour marcher droit
>   Tu chausses,
> Muse, un cothurne étroit.
> Fi du rhythme commode,
> Comme un soulier trop grand,
>   Du mode
> Que tout pied quitte et prend!
>
> . . . .
>
> Sculpte, lime, cisèle;
> Que ton rêve flottant
>   Se scelle
> Dans le bloc résistant!

The very carefully arranged lineation and emphases in these stanzas together with the highly manifest care in the choice of vocabulary all look forward to the characteristic procedure of the symbolists. This is not, of course, to suggest that Gautier was one of the symbolist poets. He does not confine himself to their customary subject matter; he has not their metaphysical concerns. The metaphor of the poet as sculptor in the last stanza cited contrasts with the habitual symbolist association of the art of the poet with that of the musician. Yet there is a larger nineteenth century tradition of the careful, lapidary crafting of language of which the symbolist tradition is but a part, even though in the later years of the century, the crucial and sustaining part. It encompasses Gautier and then Pound as well as Mallarmé and Eliot. Pound alludes to this tradition of dedicated attention to the medium in an essay which Eliot published in the *Criterion* of July 1932. He writes of a period of collaboration between himself and Eliot that occurred during the time that the initial principles of imagism were being weakened and diluted in the imagist anthologies produced by Amy Lowell and her associates. (This collaboration, Pound reports, produced the carefully wrought stanzaic works, *Hugh Selwyn Mauberley* and Eliot's *Poems* of 1920.)

Mr Eliot displayed great tact, or enjoyed good fortune, in arriving in London at a particular date with a formed style of his own. He also participated in a movement to which no name has ever been given.

That is to say, at a particular date, in a particular room, two authors, neither engaged in picking the other's pocket, decided that the dilution of *vers libre,* Amygism, Lee Masterism, general floppiness had gone too far and some counter-current must be set going. Parallel situation centuries ago in China. Remedy prescribed 'Emaux et Camées' (or the Bay State Hymn Book). Rhyme and regular strophes.

Mallarmé as well as Pound and Eliot looked to Gautier as a practitioner of the economical verbal craftsmanship that should replace 'general floppiness'. Mallarmé, just as much as the imagists may be said to be committed 'to use absolutely no word that does not contribute to the presentation.' Symbolism shares with the larger tradition of modern poetry an intense concern for the ecology of language. In one way the metaphor of poetry as music and the metaphor of poetry as sculpture are tactical rather than descriptive. They both serve to raise the question of the nature and condition of the medium. This explains why there need not necessarily be any inconsistency between Verlaine's typically symbolist emphasis on 'De la musique avant toute chose' and his other earlier insistence in the rhetorical question 'Est-elle en marbre ou non, la Venus de Milo?' For all the symbolist poets the deterioration and the necessary renewal of their medium were important problems. A continuing condition of this poetic is the awareness that language as a means of human understanding and knowledge is menaced with trivialisation and reduction.

Eliot's consciousness of this precariousness of the medium pervades *Four Quartets*. It is there explicitly in his several comments on language and poetry and implicitly in the very deliberate, word by word creation of the poem. The three essays that follow consider three different aspects of this complicated and highly conscious practice of language. Such an emphasis in no way denies that Eliot's sequence of poems comes to certain realisations about, among other things, aesthetics, metaphysics and ontology. And in my concluding essay I shall attempt to take account of this particular type of writing in the work. But I shall consider it as a particular texture of language that occurs within a pattern of other textures. *Four Quartets* is only incidentally a set of propositions about time, being and knowing with which one might agree or disagree, as with say, the arguments in Heidegger's *Being and Time* published just a few years before Eliot began writing his poem. *Four Quartets* is a pattern of words created by a verbal intelligence of rare skill, sensitivity and power. Those who, like the present writer, do not accept the declared

21

ideology of the work, under-read the poem if they make the ideology the reason for rejecting it.

This distinction is a venerable one in discussions of symbolist poetry. And it is an indispensable one. At the same time there is also a need to recognise the complexities which the distinction entails. It is not simply a denial of the possibility of philosophical statement and implication in poems but an insistence on the proper subordination of such items to the larger syntax of the whole poem. *(Four Quartets* as a whole signifies more than the sum of its individual lines and sentences and is very plainly a denial of some of them.) Symbolists have habitually suggested that words, if they are properly and fully used, have properties that may invoke aspects of reality that are not apparent to our day to day verbal awareness. In his essay on Gautier of 1859 Baudelaire writes, 'There is in words, in the Word itself, something sacred that forbids our turning them into a game of chance. Handling a language with skill is to practise a kind of evocative witchcraft.'[6]

The definition of what constitutes this supra-natural reality which words may call down for their readers or hearers is what distinguishes symbolist theory from that of other poets of the modernist tradition with whom in other matters they have so much in common. That words are semantic not merely by being referential but by the textures of sound of which they are composed, by the rhythms which any two or three of them must inevitably create and by the welter of associations which any one word brings from its history as part of the history of the language are propositions that can be discovered in the writings of non-symbolist poets such as Ezra Pound, William Carlos Williams and Charles Olson. These writers also concur with the view that the proper use of language will convey to the audience a sense of realities which the restrictive, positivist notion of language keeps from

22

expression. What these writers would deny, however, and what is central to symbolist thought is that one further property of words is the capacity to evoke, however faultily and tenuously, metaphysical essences and pure ideas. This especial understanding of what is meant by purifying the language of the tribe is intimated by Mallarmé in an elaborately and demandingly phrased rhetorical question: 'What is the point, however, of converting a fact of nature, through the game of language, into its own particular, vibrating invisibility, if not to distil, without the nuisance of close or concrete reference, its pure idea.'[7]

This characteristic symbolist endeavour to evoke the metaphysical through the physical medium of language inevitably involves paradox and tension. A further and important function of the allusion to music in this poetic is that it supplies a metaphor of a way in which the gulf between human language and supra-human reality may be bridged. Mallarmé's essay 'Crise de Vers' from which I have cited a sentence, also contains this important, if extremely difficult paragraph:

Certainly I never take my seat in the concert hall without apprehending, amidst all the unexplained sublimity, some sketch of one of the poems immanent to man or their original state, all the more intelligible because unspoken and because the composer, in order to establish the great line of it, hung back from the temptation of explaining himself. Due to what is undoubtedly a writer's incorrigible prejudice, I imagine that nothing will remain unuttered, and that we are there in the face of a breaking of literary rhythms and their scattering in sensations which are close to what is articulated by the instruments,

23

that we are there to study the art of transposing them from the symphony to the Book, or simply to take back what is ours, for it is not from basic sonorities made by brass, strings and woodwind that Music and the whole of relationships subsisting in everything will emerge in clarity and plenitude but rather from the intellectual word at its apogee.[8]

The recourse to astronomy in this last word, to the notion of the word at its highest point of removal from this world serves to indicate an aspiration and a tension that are to be found in all symbolist writing. The unverbalised truths of music, so the argument runs, are ones which the poet's medium of the word, if it were fully and properly employed, could express more satisfactorily. There are two concepts of music in Mallarmé's paragraph: the sounds which one may hear in a concert hall and those 'immanent poems' of which the concert music as mediated by the instruments is but a fragmented and approximate version. This definition of reality as a music that is more musical than music is extremely difficult to comprehend. So also is the kind of language through which such reality might be expressed. Mallarmé offers a bewilderingly grand vision of what language is to achieve. Nevertheless this vision is the chief assumption of symbolism and explains many of the particular qualities of symbolist writing. It explains, for instance, that very pronounced sense of verbal strain which we encounter both in *Four Quartets* and in Mallarmé's work. The 'grande oeuvre' which Mallarmé envisioned, the extension of symphonic truths into the yet more accurate and encompassing truths of a Book was hardly even begun. It remained only a 'might have been'. 'The whole of my admiration,' he once wrote 'goes to the great Magus,

24

inconsolable and obstinate seeker after a mystery which he does not know exists and which he will pursue for ever on that account with the affliction of his lucid despair, for it would have been the truth...' The poems that Mallarmé did write are preliminary exercises in this larger endeavour. Yet the high verbal tension in them is evidence of the poet's awareness of attempting the task of using language to break through to a reality from which language in recent custom has been removed. The very same aspiration marks the language of *Four Quartets*. Here also the 'might have been' is a key concern and reference which demands for its realisation and explication an unremitting effort to renew and develop the language.

Mallarmé was never able even to begin to realise his ambition of converting symphonic forms into words. It is Eliot's distinction within the symbolist tradition to have taken the metaphor of music and to have further specified it in such a way as to make it more practical and manageable. Music is understood in the extremely particular form of the quartet. But even if Eliot was able to sustain and complete a major work by employing and limiting himself to this form, the language of the poem, its only fleeting successes and its several failures demonstrate the extremity and the difficulty of the enterprise. For all its apparent control and pattern *Four Quartets* contains evidence of the unproductive struggle and of failure to understand reality through words. The poem conveys a strong sense that the poet and the reader are at the farthest extremes of the verbal consciousness. Language using is, in fact, one of the chief experiences presented in the poem. Associated with the struggle at the limits of language are those other issues of experience with which the poem is concerned, solipsism, the nature of the self and shifting, unstable perceptions of reality.

The theme of language use is what I shall emphasise in this book. In the final essay, for instance, in which I trace the recurrent and very much symbolist endeavour to achieve statements about ontology I shall consider the words of the poem and all that they convey rather than the ideas. I shall not attempt to extrapolate what might be supposed to be Eliot's views on the nature of being. In isolation a statement such as 'You are the music while the music lasts' is but a mystification. And an anthology of such statements about being in the poem can only aggravate the difficulty. More appropriate, more relevant to the specifically poetic enterprise of the poem than a summary of opinions is the poet's actual section by section struggle to establish the copula within the succession of words that recurrently moves from the description of perceptions and experiences to the wording of resultant states of consciousness. The third essay is a study of a sequence of verbal textures which constitute not a definition but an experiential realisation or suggestion of what being is.

The second essay is a study of the several experiences that are presented and interpreted in the poem. It does not attempt to categorise the quartets as autobiography any more than the final essay attempts to define them as philosophical statement. Yet unquestionably *Four Quartets* reports very intense personal experiences: joy, humiliation, pain and hope. Also and pervasively it presents the experience of trying to recall, present and interpret such experiences through the medium of words. It raises the question of the extent to which a recalled experience is particular to the self and the extent to which its recollection in the public, historical medium of language renders it no longer private. The poem assesses the reality of the experiences which it recalls and the possibility of communicating them. In the *Quartets,* as in so many of the poems of Mallarmé, the sense of the reality and of the recover-

26

ability of experience remembered shifts continually and often disconcertingly.

Any one of the experiences treated in the poem can only be understood in terms of a memory and a language that is affected and informed by other experiences. In its development the poem establishes a way in which experiences may be related to each other in order to make them individually and collectively intelligible. It is essentially a binary pattern and functions in a way that is similar to the sonata principle in music. In the second essay one of my purposes will be to trace the organising and collating of experience in terms of this tradition of form. Though this may seem at first sight to be an abandonment of the kind of non a priori critical procedures which I have been urging for the correct appreciation of the poem, it is also a necessary way of understanding the special verbal methods of the *Quartets* and of the major tradition in art from which they derive. If, like most major symbolist poems, *Four Quartets* is about the frontiers of consciousness, the frontiers are with a reality for which music is the most helpful metaphor. One way in which Eliot's poem marks a development from the work of Mallarmé is that it makes a general allusion not to music but rather to a precise and definite form in music which we know to have originated at a fairly definite point in history and to have developed its own character, range and achievements. The particular musical qualities of the poem are established from the very outset in the title. And the importance of the titular metaphor is recalled and sustained in the text from first to last in 'the stillness of the violin while the note lasts' in 'Burnt Norton' and in 'the complete consort' in 'Little Gidding'. And though it is difficult to delimit the precise extent of the implications of the quartet metaphor, it is clear that certain basic attributes of this form determine the organisation of *Four Quartets*. And the sonata

27

principle which is the original and principal feature of this form in music also constitutes the underlying pattern of Eliot's four poems.

The string quartet is one of the several forms deriving from the sonata principle which established itself in the course of the eighteenth century. It was before all else a principle for the expression and the reconciliation of opposites in experience and feeling. One historian notes the similarity between the binary form of sonata and the notion of dialectic which Hegel developed not so very long after. Philip Barford suggests that

> the rise and establishment of the sonata-principle corresponded in the most intimate way with the gradual emergence and full flowering of a comprehensive metaphysical system which, in so many respects, is the ultimate rationale of the logic of the sonata-principle. Ideally, one has a wordless insight into this profound and subtle matter; in words one can do little more than employ the language of analogy. The Hegelian system, at its finest, is a superb justification of the sonata-principle. Similarly, the classical sonata, at its finest, is a sensuous embodiment of the dialectical relationship of opposed terms. In the collective consciousness of late eighteenth-century man, some vital force was at work which found expression in the music, literature and philosophy—in Haydn, Mozart and Beethoven, in Goethe, in Hegel. It was the same force. It found diverse expressions.[9]

There are several reminders of this German tradition in *Four Quartets*. There is the notion of *Erhebung* which is resorted to in 'Burnt Norton' and there is the meditation on the pattern and processes of history in 'Little Gidding' which, at the time that Nazi bombs are falling upon London, is able to recall older, more civilised forms of German historical theory. But by far the most important and illuminating reference to this cultural tradition is that to the late quartets of Beethoven which were composed between 1824 and 1826. This allusion, the evidence for which lies outside the poem, serves to establish the sheer weight and ambitiousness of Eliot's enterprise in this work.[10] The level of aspiration implied is an extremely high one. J. W. N. Sullivan, for instance, in his sober and closely argued critical study of Beethoven commits himself to the following superlative and sweeping assessment of these late compositions: 'The last quartets testify to a veritable growth of consciousness, to a higher degree of consciousness, probably, than is manifested anywhere else in art.'[11]

The comparison which Eliot invites is a daring one and requires that we look closely and attentively at the scale and the nature of the experiences presented in the poem. At the same time it also compels us to investigate further the sonata principle through which the experiences are organised and understood. The notion of the relationship of opposed terms will have to be extended to include the numerous and always subtle versions, variations and developments in feeling which are to be found in the poem. The following description of sonata principle mentions some of these further implications which are plainly present in Four Quartets and which I shall consider in the second essay:

The sonata-cycle is an anti-tragic form which attempts to rise above the tragic situation through its inevitable and Utopian finale. The sonata cycle affirms the happy ending, lends itself to reconciliation, to salvation from first and second movement strivings, torments, inner doubts, and from third movement Dionysian (Scherzo) or Arcadian-aristocratic (minuet) forgetfulness. It displaces the tragic order by holding the funeral in the centre of the work, followed by rebirth and ultimately by victory, joy or peace. As in the form of Shakespearian tragedy the life cycle is complete; but the catharsis of the sonata is completed earlier; the sonata reunites the hero with society at the close (permits his rebirth, if you will), whereas the tragic form buries its protagonists.[12]

The magnitude of the themes comprehended by the sonata principle and by its derivative the quartet is also a feature of Eliot's sequence. (A misfortune in the history of the poem's reception is that it has been taken to be primarily, sometimes even exclusively, a religious or mystical work and that, as a result, its actual, highly articulated experiential range has been neglected.) The special sensuous qualities associated with the quartet form as well as its thematic range help to explain why Eliot should have resorted to it for his poetic purpose. For the connotations which this form has assumed over the two centuries of its development are very similar to the qualities which Eliot always cultivated in his own art. The compound of vitality and decorous urbanity which we find in the quartets of Haydn and Mozart and the extremities of joy and anguish expressed in Beethoven's radical revision and development of the form must undoubtedly have been a familiar and prized part of Eliot's musical culture. He may also have known of the development of the cyclical form (the use of similar material in the different movements), in the work of Debussy and César Franck which occurred at about the same time as the emergence of symbolist poetry in France. And very likely, he may have known of the major technical innovations to which the form was made susceptible in the quartets of Bartok and Schoenberg.

Yet to judge from Eliot's poem itself it is clear that more important to him than any particular instances of quartet were the particular problems of human personality, of the artist's employment of his medium and of the artist's relationship to his audience and his society which the quartet form serves to illustrate and to resolve.

Quartet form has always signified, historically, a special instance of the relationship between artist, medium and audience. One historian writes:

As the symphony was made for the listener, so the string quartet was created primarily for those who would play it. I do not mean by this that nobody was expected to listen to such pieces; but I cannot find any evidence to support the idea that large-scale quartet concerts were given in the mid-18th century. It is more likely that four expert players assembled in a fairly large room, and performed for the benefit of a few connoisseurs.[13]

The inherent tendency of quartet to be a private matter for performers culminated in the brief but highly productive association of Haydn and Mozart in Vienna in the 1780s. Important occasions in this friendship were the private concerts in which the two great composers and their gifted friends Dittersdorf and Wanhal performed their own quartets and thus figured as simultaneously authors, performers and audience of their own music.[14] In this moment of collaboration between the two great Austrian masters a form of art is endowed with an unsurpassed social coherence. It is a peculiar and memorable instance of that unity of artist, medium and audience which is such a familiar aspiration in the writings of generations of poets, from before Mallarmé to after Eliot, who must deal with the consequences of social fragmentation. This unity of the aesthetic transaction which is recalled by quartet form was admittedly a very short lived phenomenon. Later and more characteristically the quartet became a divided activity like any other. The composer wrote his music for a performer who was likely to be someone other than himself. And performers, as the practice of house music diminished in the course of the nineteenth century, made their music professionally in the concert hall. Nevertheless, as the phrase 'the music of friends' reminds us, the possibility of intimacy and unity remains an important part of the traditions of chamber music and one which is recollected in Eliot's poem. As a form that of its nature continually questions the extent of its audience, quartet has much to say that is relevant to the social, cultural and psychological situation of modern poetry. Quartet form inevitably alludes to an uncertain negotiation, a suspension between the utterly private world of the composer and the public world of the concert hall.

Eliot goes further than Mallarmé or than James Joyce in his *Chamber Music* in recruiting to his poetic method the particulars of a specific musical form as these have evolved historically. Eliot's music is not just verbal sound. Structurally and psychologically it is far more complex. By virtue of its four part nature the quartet inevitably raises the issue of unity and diversity in perception. A quartet offers four versions, four representations of feeling which it is the function of the form to bring together in one. Eliot, as both his poetry

32

and his prose suggest, was not a writer who employed a single voice unselfconsciously and easily. More so than many other poets of this century who felt compelled to resort to mask, role and persona, Eliot was a poet of many voices, one who was sensitively aware of the fact of his several verbal roles and identities. To concede the authenticity of these verbal fragmentations of the self and at the same time to encompass them at the last in a unity was a necessary enterprise for which the quartet form could serve better than any other as model. What the poet writes are pre-eminently parts which his several voices perform. And he writes them in such a way that we find ourselves listening with him and, as the performance progresses, judging, criticising the tone and implications of a particular voice, group of voices or movement. To trace out the 'four in one' unity of *Four Quartets* is to understand the way in which its particular musical form is a double therapeutic. It contains the divisions and fragmentations of the poet's language and at the same time promotes (and this is an important subject of the poem) the true unity and integrity of the self. The fourfold unity of the authorial self predicated by the quartet form is the subject of the first of the following essays on the musical semantics of *Four Quartets*.

One

One

Towards the end of his life Mallarmé compared the function of the writer with that of the actor or (if the lesser status connoted by the word 'histrion' is to be suggested) of the player. 'The writer,' he maintained in an essay published in 1895, 'must establish himself in the text as the spiritual actor whether of a happiness or of his sufferings...'[15] The chief implication of this metaphor has to do with the poet's employment of his medium. He does not, the suggestion runs, use language spontaneously and unreflectingly; he rather manages it carefully and consciously in order to subserve and to arrive at a desired effect. He is not verbally autonomous, he is the instrument of and for something else. This idea of the poet as performer is also cognate with the symbolist metaphor of poetry as music. In this tradition of thought the poet, like the concert performer, is there to read and transmit certain feelings, patterns and formulations of reality.

Such a theory of the poet's function necessarily entails a relegation of the poet's own character and personality. He is but the poor player. In a well known letter Rimbaud spoke of the experience in which 'Je est un autre'. And this surrendering of the self and a readiness to assume and to act other selves is a persistent feature of the symbolist tradition.

It explains the prominence of the dramatic monologue in the work of its members. *Le Bateau Ivre, L'Après Midi d'un Faune,* and *The Love Song of J. Alfred Prufrock* are all enactments of self. They show the poet striving to allow someone other than himself to come into being. As with the concert artist there is a tension between performer and performed. The definition and authenticity of both are perpetually in question.

If the dramatic monologue is habitual with the symbolists, it is not, of course, peculiar to them. Instances of the form can be found as early as the 1840s in the work of Tennyson and of Browning. Robert Langbaum suggests that this kind of poem is 'an appropriate form for an empirical and relativist age'.[16] It allows the poet to essay and to test a variety of styles and points of view that become available in an increasingly articulated age. The issue of whether the self can or should be integral or polymorphous is not exclusively a concern of the nineteenth century. It is a very ancient question. But it does assume a particular urgency and develop new forms during this period. Tennyson, Browning and Mallarmé write dramatic monologues; Dr Johnson does not. Clearly the emergence of this particular form some sixty years or so after Dr Johnson's death has something to do with the developing social, intellectual and moral pluralism of those years. The influential concept of alienation which Hegel proposed during this period is a linguistic and thus literary as well as a social matter.

The classical string quartet is another of the forms that were established at this time. It is also predicated on the multiplicity of the self. A principal characteristic of the classical quartet form as this was developed by Haydn in the 1770s and the 1780s was an equal interchange between the four instruments. In Haydn's quartets of these years the two older forms of four part music, a succession of solo parts or an essentially orchestral writing were replaced by a form

38

which allows for contrast, tension, debate and discussion among the instruments. This property of the classical quartet form is one of the clear implications of Eliot's titular metaphor. There are four voices in his poem and, since they are very much voices for social performance, the principle of instrumentality asserts itself as strongly in this writing as in the musical form itself. And the fact that there are four parts, four voices, means that each individual one is only a version. The full account, the complete version is the sum and interaction of all four performances.

Four Quartets comprises four dramatic monologues which interweave and combine but which always remain recognisable. The four verbal roles which we hear may be described as those of the lecturer, the prophet, the conversationalist and the conjuror. The rapid and complex interaction of these four voices and the unmistakeable inference that there is a distinction to be made between the poet and his four verbal instruments account for that unremitting intricacy of tone which constitutes much of the meaning and achievement of the poem.

As with a musical instrument each voice in the poem has its own range. That of the lecturer, for instance, can be heard to move from the quiet meditative speculation of the opening lines to the somewhat bullying, insistent explanation of the significance of Little Gidding in the opening movement of that quartet. Each range is such that the four basic descriptions cannot be employed rigidly. The conjuror at one time sounds like a stage hypnotist and at another like a sorcerer with more than merely human skills. The seer voices both cosmic prophecies and private anxieties. The lecturer sometimes addresses us with a studied care and sometimes succumbs to platitudes and to the journalese. The four categories are not absolutes. Each voice constitutes a certain attitude to reality that contains within it a wide variety of possible emphases. And sometimes the voices sound together in passages of trio, duet or quartet. This kind of tonal combination is also an important semantic feature in the development of the poem.

To trace all the groupings of the voices or even all the passages for the individual voice would be a very lengthy undertaking. And it would be extremely difficult to give a fully detailed account of their numerous and complex modulations. In this essay, in order to suggest something of this important but neglected aspect of the poem, I shall attempt to propose a general summary of its tonal development.

The first four sentences of the poem are spoken in the voice of the lecturer pondering a hypothesis on the incorrigibility of time. The tone is one that conveys a sense of a wearying, defeating banality. At the eleventh line a second voice enters, one that replaces the slow meditative emphases of the earlier lines with a new quickness. The grinding abstractions give way to interesting concrete nouns. The echoing footfalls and the unopened door create a mood of mystery and excitement that belong to the world of the stage magician who soon identifies himself with a familiar verbal gesture:

My words echo
Thus, in your mind.

The suggestion of the stage hypnotist putting his subject to sleep in order to give him an altogether new sense of reality is confirmed and intensified by the lineation. (In *Four Quartets* just as in the work of William Carlos Williams or Charles Olson the lineating of words serves as an important semantic

40

device.) Here the breaking of the line effects a deceleration and a mesmerising intensity. The particular stress that is made to fall upon the word 'Thus' requires us to think of difficult analogies and different forms of reality. The conjuror then speedily completes his work. We are introduced into a world that is far removed from that of abstract speculation, a fairy tale world of talking birds, invisible people and mysterious gardens.

In the subsequent description of the rose garden experience the voice of the conjuror modulates imperceptibly into that of the conversationalist who relates the occurrence in the manner of a nursery tale. The voice is that of one speaking simply and yet formally to children. It is measured and controlled as it describes the world of make-believe but it is also marked by a throb of laughter and joy as it speaks of the dance and of the unheard music. There is in these lines a scherzo quality, the sense of a profoundly entertaining and successful joke which for all its hugeness of scale and complexity of manifestation is gravely sustained by its participants.

Five lines from the end of the movement the reader is banished from the world summoned by the conjuror. We awake to the very same words spoken by the lecturer which we were hearing some thirty lines earlier:

What might have been and what has been
Point to one end, which is always present.

But the force of these words has now changed. On the earlier occasion, as part of the abstract meditation, these lines conveyed a view of time as something deadly banal. Now, after the experience of following the echoes in the rose garden,

41

these other echoing words take on altogether new resonance and implication. The words are exactly the same but their meanings have significantly altered. 'End' no longer means a sterile termination but a valid and valuable purpose. 'Present' no longer signifies a depressing irremediable now but alludes to the presence of a world of excitement and happiness that may be conjured and recalled to human consciousness. The conjuror's language has affected the language of adult analytical intelligence. An important method of the poem is clearly established. This renewal of the two lines in their recapitulation at the end of this first movement is an excellent instance of the sonata design of the *Quartets*.

The second movement of 'Burnt Norton' is tonally less complex than the first. The opening fifteen lines are the seer's response to the experience in the garden. They are an acceleratingly rapturous celebration of a vision of a unity underlying disparate and conflicting experience. In the second section the voice of the lecturer is heard again. He attempts to explain the significance of the experience in the abstract and sometimes technical terms of the philosopher. This endeavour, as the syntactical uncertainty suggests, is problematical and finally unavailing. Twelve lines from the end the seer intervenes to speak more effectively and conclusively of the matter. The final two sentences are spoken by the conversationalist who supplements the words of the seer by referring modestly and quietly to specific human realities:

To be conscious is not to be in time
But only in time can the moment in the rose-garden,
The moment in the arbour where the rain beat,
The moment in the draughty church at smokefall
Be remembered; . . . .

42

After the essays in abstract and abstruse interpretation these last lines return the movement to concrete realities.

At the opening of the middle movement of 'Burnt Norton' the voices of the seer and lecturer sound together. It is as though they have returned yet again to the task of trying to formulate the major experience of the poem in their own terms. One of the main tensions of the sequence is the struggle of these two kinds of sophisticated consciousness to assimilate experience to their particular verbal styles. Words such as eructation and plenitude establish the tone of a carefully specified clinical diagnosis which we associate with the lecturing voice. But the pitying, magisterial scorn which pervades the writing here belongs clearly to the seer who, at the twenty fifth line, after the division of the movement speaks alone for some eleven lines and urges the reader in the words and phrases of St. John of the Cross, to strive to liberate himself from the futile continuum of 'Time before and time after'.

The brief fourth movement is also an exchange between two voices. The first three sentences are of a modestly colloquial kind. The first registers the dismal realisation that the experience in the rose garden is now past. The next two are a succession of hasty, anxious questions about what is to happen next. The child-like tone of these lines recalls that nursery conversation in the first movement. But the final sentence which is an answer to the questioning has the decisive tone of the seer:

After the kingfisher's wing
Has answered light to light, and is silent, the light is
still

At the still point of the turning world.

The notion of stillness introduced in this fourth section is the conceptual conclusion of 'Burnt Norton'. The fifth and final movement is really only a discursive explanation of the particular enterprise of the poem, the endeavour to represent stillness in a pattern of words. The lecturer moves confidently to his task until the fourth sentence in which syntax is defeated by paradox and mystery. A renewed effort (at the thirteenth line) to comment on the nature of words is again subverted by imagistic musing:

> The crying shadow in the funeral dance,
> The loud lament of the disconsolate chimera.

There is here an incompatibility between a coherent public rhetoric and the distractions of private images.

After the division in the movement the expansive lineation gives way to a much shorter line that suggests a lecturer who is retreating to curt note form. The musing into which the lecturer had fallen at the end of the opening section is criticised by these brief new lines. The speaker returns to his original subject, pattern. But yet again the attempt at discursive formulation is terminated by the upsurging, quickening memory of the experience which is both the origin and the example of the lecturer's discourse:

> Sudden in a shaft of sunlight
> Even while the dust moves
> There rises the hidden laughter
> Of children in the foliage
> Quick now, here, now, always—.

44

In this way the poem ends with one more demonstration of the tension between the voice that speaks of private, visionary experience and the voice which attempts to speak a public truth.

The opening section of 'East Coker' contains parts for all four voices. The tone of the opening lines suggests a lingering, more detailed contemplation of 'the waste sad time', the wearying cyclical succession of temporal processes. It is spoken, pre-eminently by the prophetic voice that easily resorts to an echoing of words from Ecclesiastes. But the conversational voice is also there to set the scene in a more prosaic, contemporary England:

>   Now the light falls
> Across the open field, leaving the deep lane
> Shuttered with branches, dark in the afternoon,
> Where you lean against a bank while a van passes,
> And the deep lane insists on the direction
> Into the village, in the electric heat
> Hypnotised.

The hypnotic somnolence which informs the ending of this sentence is different from the hypnotic state brought about by the conjuror in 'Burnt Norton'. The mood here is that of a dull cynical complacency. But again the conjuror enters to create a new image of temporal experience. As at the corresponding point in the earlier quartet his cautionary voice is heard introducing a trick to an audience of children:

> In that open field
> If you do not come too close, if you do not come
> > too close,
> On a summer midnight, you can hear the music
> Of the weak pipe and the little drum
> And see them dancing around the bonfire.

The vision is realised and the people from the past made to appear before us. But this time the conjured reality has no vivifying effect. At the last the country dancers and their rhythms merely corroborate the earlier sense of the wearying, even distasteful repetitions of mundane time:

> The time of milking and the time of harvest
> The time of the coupling of man and woman
> And that of beasts. Feet rising and falling.
> Eating and drinking. Dung and death.

The vision elicits from the seer who can be heard entering at the end only boredom and disgust at the processes of human life and history. The kind of human feeling and understanding suggested by the movement and pattern of the rural dance (one of the important origins and persistent features of the string quartet form) is at this stage in the poem definitely repudiated.

The second movement is also initiated by the seer. But his words immediately convey a disturbing, radical change in his outlook, mood and style. The passage begins with a long, seven line question, the dominant tone of which is one of breathless surprise. The temporal pattern of mundane life which earlier he had described so confidently and even cynically is now most shockingly invalidated. World weariness here vanishes before an unexpected prospect of violence, destruction and apocalypse.

The second part of this movement is spoken by the voice of the conversationalist:

> That was a way of putting it—not very satisfactory:
> A periphrastic study in a worn-out poetical fashion.

This is the first clear instance in the sequence of the way in which Eliot's quartet method enables one voice to criticize another. Here the more humble, colloquial voice judges the prophetic style of the seer and also (by implication) the seer's vision and reliability. *Four Quartets* ultimately confirms the role of the seer but in its course of development the poem clearly demonstrates the difficulties attending the prophetic style and function in the present phase of history, culture and language.

The conversational discussion of the prophet's failure modulates questioningly into an editorialising summary from the lecturer:

> There is, it seems to
> us,
> At best, only a limited value
> In the knowledge derived from experience.
> The knowledge imposes a pattern, and falsifies.

Then follow some new realisations on the part of the seer

himself who now employs a language that conveys an awareness of fear and of loneliness and also a new humility:

> And every moment is a new and shocking
> Valuation of all we have been. We are only undeceived
> Of that which, deceiving, could no longer harm.
> In the middle, not only in the middle of the way
> But all the way, in a dark wood, in a bramble,
> On the edge of a grimpen, where is no secure foothold,
> And menaced by monsters, fancy lights,
> Risking enchantment.

Each movement in 'East Coker' forms a pronounced tonal contrast with the corresponding one in 'Burnt Norton'. The massive contempt for metropolitan civilisation deployed in the third section of the earlier quartet is here extended by a passage that carries a greater intensity both of mockery and of involvement. The tedious roster of the titles, functions and reference books of modern social life is accompanied by the more difficult realisation that 'we all go with them'. The disdainful aloofness of 'Burnt Norton' is no longer possible after the recent shocking conviction of inadequate and partial understanding. 'The wisdom of old men' has been brought into question and one part of the seer's dissociation of himself from that wisdom is a movement from the ideas and activities associated with the 'we' to a psychological and spiritual cure undertaken solely by the 'I'. An important tonal dialectic in the *Quartets* is that involving the pronouns. In the spirit of the first of the epigraphs from Heraclitus the 'I' continually searches for the larger wisdom that is voiced by the 'we'. But one of the recognitions of the poem is that the use of 'we' may entail inadequate, improper or compromising solidarities.

After prescribing to himself 'Wait without thought, for you are not ready for thought', the seer again attempts his task of supplying visionary exhortation. But he no longer possesses his former confidence. His prophesying is prefaced by nervous, uncertain exchange with the reader:

> You say I am repeating
> Something I have said before. I shall say it again.
> Shall I say it again?

The dozen lines with which this third section ends are, as at the same point in 'Burnt Norton', an adaptation of some words of St. John of the Cross. But in the context of the experience of this quartet they assume a new quality of nervous insistence and urgency. The experience of radical misjudgement, uncertainty and instability is what may also explain the seeming verbal crudity of the fourth movement which begins:

> The wounded surgeon plies the steel
> That questions the distempered part;
> Beneath the bleeding hands we feel
> The sharp compassion of the healer's art
> Resolving the enigma of the fever chart.

The first five stanzas of this movement comprise a virtuoso account of Christianity in terms of a blatant symbolism that conveys the impression of a headlong desire to return to

49

fundamental unshakeable truths, however unpleasant or distasteful, however much a reductive caricature of the poet's best awareness they may be.

In the final movement this tendency to a certain emotional imbalance abates. The first eleven lines serve to establish a relaxed conversational intimacy with the reader:

> So here I am, in the middle way, having had twenty years—
> Twenty years largely wasted, the years of *l'entre deux*
> > *guerres*
> Trying to learn to use words . . .

The nervous insistence and the self laceration of the preceding movement are now abandoned. The conversation clearly implies a criticism of the preceding movement. The corrected prophecies of the seer prove to have been imperfectly managed and the quartet returns to the more genuine simplicity and the humane unpretentiousness of the conversationalist.

The second half of the movement turns to the difficult task of summing up the painful and complicated experiences presented in the quartet. It sounds as though spoken principally by the voice of the conversationalist with some accompaniment from the lecturer. The modest public style of these last lines advances the concept of a 'lifetime burning in every moment' as an explanation of 'that destructive fire' which had reduced to nothing the seer's prophecies earlier in the poem. The concept expressly recalls the bonfire around which the villagers of East Coker had danced. Ordinary, historical humanity had a way, the conversationalist now realises and appreciates, of managing and patterning this elemental fact of life which the once presumptuous seer did not. Only after the kindly articulating of this realisation does the voice of the seer return to speak the concluding two or three sentences contritely and quietly. The wisdom of old men requires redefinition:

Old men ought to be explorers
Here or there does not matter
We must be still and still moving
Into another intensity
For a further union, a deeper communion
Through the dark cold and the empty desolation,
The wave cry, the wind cry, the vast waters
Of the petrel and the porpoise. In my end is my beginning.

'East Coker' proves to be a poem about the education of the prophetic voice and style. And the four part tonal structure of the sequence, it is now apparent, is no mere technical device. It is the inevitable expression of the basic subject matter of the poems. The author of the work is not just one voice, nor does he apprehend reality in one way, nor does he talk about it in one verbal style. He is a set of different, sometimes insufficient, sometimes contradictory perceptions and his modes of language vary. The poem may be defined as a process of investigation, of exploration into the nature of the self. And the initial, formal assumption is that the self is a plurality. The notion is very similar to the one which we find at the centre of one of the great historical accounts and phases of the divided consciousness, that represented by Diderot's *Le Neveu de Rameau*. As Lionel Trilling reminds us in his *Sincerity and Authenticity* Diderot's book had great appeal for a whole succession of writers who studied man's alienation

51

from his society, his culture and himself.[17] It was alluded to admiringly by Hegel, by Marx and by Freud. And the main assumption of this work recurs as the main assumption of Eliot's *Four Quartets*. The chief point that the poor and unsuccessful nephew of the great composer insists upon in his dialogue with Diderot is that everyone in society is constrained to perform a variety of roles. The climax of the book comes when the nephew abandons his theorising about roles and, to the shock and alarm of his interlocutor, Diderot, performs a whole opera in which he takes all the roles, sings all the parts, plays all the instruments:

He jumbled together thirty different airs, French, Italian, comic, tragic—in every style. Now in a baritone voice he sank to the pit; then straining in falsetto he tore to shreds the upper notes of some air, imitating the while the stance, walk and gestures of the several characters; being in succession furious, mollified, lordly, sneering. First a damsel weeps and he reproduces her kittenish ways; next he is a priest, a king, a tyrant . . . . Now he is a slave, he obeys, calms down, is heartbroken, complains, laughs . . . With swollen cheeks and sombre throaty sound, he would give us the horns and bassoons. For the oboes he assumed a shrill yet nasal voice, then speeded up the emission of sound to an incredible degree for the strings . . . . He whistled piccolos and warbled traverse flutes, singing, shouting, waving about like a madman, being in himself dancer and ballerina, singer and prima donna, all of them together and the whole orchestra, the whole theatre; then redividing himself into twenty separate roles, running, stopping, glowing at the eyes like one possessed, frothing at the mouth . . . .[18]

Such a performance makes Eliot's music seem very modest and quiet. It is the difference between the music of the opera and the music of the quartet. Nevertheless the two performances belong to the same tradition of thinking about the self. True selfhood for the nephew means the granting of expression to that great variety of selves within the individual of which men in his time have become aware. A full and rich humanity, for which the opera offers the image, comes from recognising and allowing all the self's voices.

It is noteworthy that Diderot's book was written, as far as is known, in the last third of the eighteenth century, at the very same time that the string quartet was becoming a recognisable form. It attests to an emergent condition of the human consciousness with which the quartet principle as practised by Hadyn, Mozart, Beethoven and much later on by Eliot is designed to contend. The realisation of a full and true selfhood is approached by means of this device of conceding and reconciling all the voices of the self, however inadequate, discordant or false any particular voice from time to time may be. 'East Coker' affords the first very audible instance of the expression and containment of such falsenesses; 'Dry Salvages' in its further, deeper analysis of consciousness entails others of a different kind.

The opening lines of this third quartet convey an impression of affectation:

I do not know much about gods; but I think that the
              river
Is a strong brown god—.

They also blatantly disregard the curative prescription made out for himself by the seer in 'East Coker': 'Wait without thought for you are not ready for thought' and also the later achieved proposition 'And what you do not know is the only thing you know'. The first few lines of 'Dry Salvages' spoken in the voice of the conversationalist appear to constitute a retreat from the best wisdom of the previous quartet. And as a piece of writing they have received strong and justifiable criticism. The first ten lines are a somewhat pompous, platitudinising restatement of the unforeseen in life that was the subject of the previous quartet. One implication of these lines is the difficulty of articulating the wisdom gained at East Coker. Neither the language of conversation nor that of the lecture is sufficient. Only in the last four lines of this opening passage in which the prophetic voice enters to evoke the unpredictable rhythms of experience in terms of convincingly specific memories does the writing become revitalised. The river is no longer an abstraction:

His rhythm was present in the nursery bedroom,
In the rank ailanthus of the April dooryard,
In the smell of grapes on the autumn table,
And the evening circle in the winter gaslight.

In the second part of the movement the seer proceeds to enlarge upon the lecturer's initial metaphor. The passage begins:

The river is within us, the sea is all about us.

This dramatic introduction of the idea of another range of human vulnerability is followed by a series of quick, vivid images of the sea and of the timelessness which it signifies. The further implications of the personal sickness and fever presented in 'East Coker' are the larger and perennial questions of the meaning of human suffering and agony. In its evocation of the endlessness of suffering, the seer's voice has an authenticity that was absent in the previous voices of the movement. This opens with another tacit comparison of the range and capacities of the voices.

The six carefully wrought stanzas that follow are a lyrical response to the new awareness defined in the first movement. These lines are a crescendo of lament uttered by all the voices. (The governing personal pronoun is 'we'.) The structure is antiphonal with the prophetic voice preponderating both in the questions and the responses.

With the subject now established in more authentic detail and in all its emotional reverberations it is possible for the lecturer in the second part of the movement to attempt again to understand the matter in discursive fashion. The tone and the writing are here less rhetorical, less flaccid than in the opening section. The several careful qualifications and the parentheses suggest the element of struggle involved in the effort to communicate the significance of Dry Salvages to the 'popular mind'. And the failure of the syntax in the second sentence again suggests the difficulty of genuinely comprehending the experience in this particular mode of language. The passage becomes more coherent and composed as it proceeds. But in the last nine lines the voice of the seer again emerges to replace the abstractions employed by the lecturer with a more conclusive language of powerful and compelling concretion:

Time the destroyer is time the preserver,
Like the river with its cargo of dead negroes,
                    cows and chicken coops,
The bitter apple and the bite in the apple.

The third movement of 'Dry Salvages' is tonally more
various than any other in *Four Quartets*. It begins with a
recourse to the conversational mode that serves to relieve the
menacing solemnity of the end of the preceding section:

I sometimes wonder if that is what Krishna meant—
Among other things—.

But the gesture is mannered and inadequate. The colloquial
mode is here insufficient and false and the passage quickly
reverts to the seer:

And the way up is the way down, the way forward is
                              the way back.
You cannot face it steadily, but this thing is sure,
That time is no healer . . . . .

The explanation of this apparent mystification is then
undertaken by the lecturer. In order to clarify what he has to
say he employs as an example passengers on a train, people
who are suspended from place and from time. But well before
this illustration has been completed the voice of the seer
breaks in to apostrophise the people who are but creatures

of the lecturer's words: 'Fare forward, travellers'. The voices
now prove to be not merely different responses to experience;
each one may be in itself an experience to which another
responds.

The tone of exalted exhortation is maintained for the next
nine lines and then there is introduced a kind of communication
that belongs as much to the world of the conjuror as to that
of the seer. It is a mysterious inexplicable voice that speaks
not to the ear and not through language:

> At nightfall, in the rigging and the aerial,
> Is a voice descanting (though not to the ear,
> The murmuring shell of time, and not in any language).

The following eighteen lines comprise the words which this
parodoxically wordless, languageless voice in fact descants
to the passengers. The quotation contains within it yet a
further quotation, some words of Krishna's in the *Bhagavad-
Gita*. There is in this passage a peculiar act of conjuring or
perhaps of ventriloquism in which the prophetic voice invokes
another and extra-sensory voice which in turn quotes from
Krishna. It recalls that other complex conjuring act at Burnt
Norton in which a sense of a world beyond the phenomenal
was made available briefly to perception. And the co-operation
of the prophet and the conjuror illustrates the degree of
similarity between them in their modes of acting upon reality.

The prayer to the Virgin Mary which constitutes the fourth
movement quickly and unassumingly confirms the seer's
Christian categorisations of the metaphysical realm to which
he looks. The tone here is a compound of humility, simplicity
and compassion. It serves to make more intelligible and

more human the ideological devices to which the poem resorts as a means of explaining suffering: the shifting of the word annunciation from the lower to the higher case in the second section and the dramatic introduction of the concept of Incarnation in the final movement.

The first nineteen lines of this conclusion are voiced by the lecturer who now speaks with a poise, a trenchancy and a syntactical control that are not to be found in the two preceding passages spoken by this voice in 'Dry Salvages'. A main process in this poem is the education of the discursive voice into a better, more accurate manner of talking about suffering. In 'East Coker' the prophetic voice underwent experience and tonal development; in 'Dry Salvages' the voice is that of the teacher.

At the twentieth line the voice of the seer re-enters to add a qualification to what the lecturer has said about sanctity. The seer goes on to recall other moments 'in and out of time' and is suddenly accompanied by a voice that recalls the conjuring of the mysterious descant in the previous section. It speaks of

> music heard so deeply
> That it is not heard at all, but you are the music
> While the music lasts.

The poem closes with some eighteen lines in which all four voices may be heard uttering a prospect of human contentment. The poem has worked its way from the false tonality of the 'I' of the opening lines of the quartet to the more textured and convincing first person plural of the close.

58

'Little Gidding' opens with the voice of the seer accompanied, very subduedly at the outset, by that of the lecturer. The first twenty lines move from a dispassionate exploration of the phenomenon 'midwinter spring' to a suggestion of present, actual involvement in it in simultaneously meteorological and psychological terms, 'In windless cold that is the heart's heat'. The voice of the lecturer always implies a distancing from the object, whereas that of the seer communicates its vibrant presence.

The moment of wondering rapture is abruptly terminated and there begins a passage, part conversational, part pedantically lecturing that considers what an ordinary visit to Little Gidding, rather than this very extraordinary one, would be like. The repetition of the word 'likely' and the mundane details of the place, the pig sty, the dull façade and the tombstone all help to emphasise this contrast between the normal and the abnormal. In the third section the voice of the lecturer emerges very distinctly and with a bullying quality to it, to instruct the reader about the significance of a place such as this, 'Where prayer has been valid'. In the third as in the second section of this first movement the repetitions suggest a nervous anxiety about placing this new experience in its full and correct context. There is a slightly strident determination to avoid the failure of interpretation that had occurred at Burnt Norton.

The first half of the second movement is made up of three eight line stanzas in which the seer quietly laments the mortality of the phenomenal world and of the elements of which it is composed. The images in these lines, 'Dust in the air suspended' and 'the parched eviscerate soil' derive from the bombing of London in 1941. The weary slowness of the short lines and the heaviness of the rhymes convey the hopelessness of the prophet's vision here. As Raymond Preston has said, 'There is nothing so positive here as a vision of the Last Day. There is only utter negation, a spiritual despair which the whole of the rest of the poem fights . . .'[19]

The second portion of this movement is a pendant and a contrast to the first. The rhythm quickens and the lines lengthen. The seer describes a vision, or hallucination, that occurred one morning at dawn during the time of the London Blitz. The narrative manner is very deliberate and formal. Along with the elevated, somewhat Augustan manner of the seer, so different from his earlier dull despair, there may be heard occasional, light accompaniment from the other three voices. The visionary encounter is at one moment presented in words that suggest that the conjuror is performing a ventriloquist's trick:

So I assumed a double part, and cried
And heard another's voice cry: 'What! are *you* here?'

And the last few lines make it clear that the encounter is at its simplest a matter of conversation. Later on as the dead mentor lists and explains the three conditions 'To set a crown upon your lifetime's effort', the lines sound as though they are being performed by the lecturer. Nevertheless, despite these more mundane versions of the experience, this section is pre-eminently prophetic. Its recognition in bombed London and in the experience of the individual both of nothingness (a recurrent theme in Mallarmé's writing) and of the restoration from the pain which results from such an awareness is the most important and verbally the richest and densest passage for the prophetic voice in the whole sequence. The weighty, yet calm, almost virtuoso control of the complex syntax and unusual and paradoxical wording contribute to the prominence which this section enjoys, not only within 'Little Gidding' but within the complete sequence of the quartets. The passage is, as I will suggest in the following essay, the culmination of the pattern of experiences which the poem organises. But it is also the actual instance of the ideal of every phrase and sentence that is right with which the poem concludes. This particular verbal quality is made all the more conspicuous by the verbal and syntactical labouring and by the failures that occur in earlier quartets.

The first line of the third section sounds like a medical lecture. The curative wisdom which may be learned from the past and from the dead is what the lecturer sets out to define. But his attempt comes quickly to sound premature and insufficient. For, though he begins with a gesture that suggests pedagogical confidence and control ('There are three conditions which often look alike/Yet differ completely'), the rest of the sentence degenerates into a collection of poorly related phrases that belie the smoothly coherent understanding that had been intimated. The next two sentences are also unsure. The explanation is at last interrupted by the conjuror who intervenes to offer a demonstration. His characteristic patter alludes to that vanishing act which constitutes the relation of present and past and of living and dead, an act which, as we have just seen in the case of the 'dead master', may disrupt the normal world of appearances:

See, now they vanish,
The faces and places, with the self which, as it could,
loved them,
To become renewed, transfigured, in another pattern.

The voice of the seer which re-enters at the next line proceeds to develop and celebrate this notion of larger, unfamiliar temporal perspectives by invoking some lines from the four-teenth century mystic Dame Julian of Norwich. And the remain-ing thirty or so lines are part lecture, part conversation in which the explanation of history as a patterning of the dead is further elaborated. 'Little Gidding' recalls men of the seventeenth century who in life opposed each other but who in death, 'are folded in a single party'. In death they exist in our memory in a coherence of which they were unaware in life: they 'Accept the constitution of silence'. In this third section of the quartet Eliot returns discursively to the experience in 'this place' that had been presented in the first section. Lecturer and seer refer to the experiences of historical people in this place and to the subsequent, present effect of these experiences as a further illustration of that new knowledge of time which is 'midwinter spring'. Part of this, it is now suggested, is an understanding of 'the communication of the dead'. The full explanation has been deferred until now in order to allow for the presentation of the communication of the dead master in London which forms a contrast with the communication at Little Gidding. These two experiences sustain the simple and homely words from Dame Julian which are repeated at the end of the movement.

The fourteen lines of the fourth movement have the sound of a highly charged prophetic vision. The passage intervenes between the quick short lines of confident explanation with which the third movement ends and the calmly expansive, longer lines of more general statement that open the final movement. The second of the two stanzas introduces the voice of the lecturer or perhaps the conversationalist raising the question of the origins of human suffering. The question is answered with a massive monosyllabic confidence. Despite the presence of these less intense voices, the movement as a whole has not so much the quality of discourse as of concentrated prophetic summation.

The fifth and final movement in a conversational tone of sympathetic human feeling initiates a discussion of ends and beginnings that also accommodates a long and still pleasantly colloquial parenthesis on words and poetry. Next the conjuror enters to perform his characteristic act of making visible to us the usually invisible continuities between ends and beginnings, past and future, living and dead, perhaps even, the poet and his reputation:

> We die with the dying:
> See, they depart, and we go with them.
> We are born with the dead:
> See, they return, and bring us with them.

Then enters the voice of the prophet who pronounces three weighty and sonorous sentences. The first is an allegorical summation of the poem, the second a proposition concerning man's essentially historical nature and the third a statement of what history is in terms of the experience at Little Gidding and all that experience has brought to mind by way of associations and understanding.

The single isolated line quoted from *The Cloud of Unknowing*, 'With the drawing of this Love and the voice of this Calling', is another instance of historical echoing, an instance which both in its origins and in its use of the higher case alludes to yet further removes in history than those with which the quartet has been principally concerned.

The main feature of the concluding section is a nine line

63

sentence that ends with a recollection of that moment of conjured delight that occurred at the very beginning, at Burnt Norton:

> Through the unknown, remembered gate
> When the last of earth left to discover
> Is that which was the beginning;
> At the source of the longest river
> The voice of the hidden waterfall
> And the children in the apple-tree
> Not known, because not looked for
> But heard, half-heard, in the stillness
> Between two waves of the sea.

The other three voices of the quartet can also be heard in these final twenty lines. For if they recall the initial sorcery, they are also conversational, informative and visionary. It is as though here, at the last, the four voices which have undergone conflict, struggle and individual development, sound together in their own best and most educated terms in that unity towards which the quartet form characteristically aspires.

Two

Two

For all the musical procedures that are implied in the title of *Four Quartets* and realised in its section by section development, Eliot's work remains a poem, which is to say that, since words are characteristically more referential than musical sounds, it is *about* something, that it has a subject, that it describes and interprets certain experiences. Yet to state plainly what these experiences are is no simple task. This is in great part because the poem in its ever shifting tones and modes continually calls in question the reality of what is presented as experience. The consciousness predicated by the four voices of the quartets can no more give certain descriptions of what has impinged upon it than it can supply and confidently state its own identity.

The kind of scepticism about the nature of experience which we find in *Four Quartets* is very much a feature of the twentieth century mind. It is one of the things that makes the poem so manifestly a work of modernism. Walter Benjamin gives a succinct account of the origins of such questioning. He writes:

... experience has fallen in value. And it looks as if it is continuing to fall into bottomlessness. Every glance at a newspaper demonstrates that it has reached a new low, that our picture not only of the external world but of the moral world as well, overnight has undergone changes which were never thought possible. With the First World War a process began to become apparent which has not halted since then . . . For never has experience been contradicted more thoroughly than strategic experience by tactical warfare, economic experience by inflation, bodily experience by mechanical warfare, moral experience by those in power.[20]

Uncertainty about the reliable actuality of experience begins with the presentation of the very first occurrence that is described in the sequence, the moment of happiness and exaltation in the rose garden at Burnt Norton. Since it is such a commanding reference point in this quartet and also in the following ones, the event is allowed by the reader to have been an actual one. Yet at the same time the many literary and mythical associations which the description contains make it also appear to be a construct or synthesis. It seems possible to say of it what J. W. N. Sullivan said of a passage in Beethoven's Fourth Symphony:

We need not suppose that any actual love experience inspired the slow movement of this symphony. The state depicted could well exist without an object. Indeed, there is a certain deliberateness, a sort of formality, about this movement, that suggests a purely imaginative realisation of the state depicted. It is the expression of a romantic dream, and in its controlled and shapely loveliness it lacks the poignancy of a definite individual experience.[21]

The doubt about whether the experience in the rose garden is real or imaginary, actual or vicarious, personal or literary, applies to other experiences presented later in the quartets. It may even be said, perhaps, that such uncertainty is itself one of the experiences, an all pervading experience that is conveyed by the poem. Undoubtedly in the description of the experience in the rose garden there are allusions that direct us to an ancient mythical version of the questions about the reality of experience, of the extent of solipsism and of the genuineness of that which is thought to be external to the self. The staring down into a pool in a place inhabited by echoes and the entrancing reflection of beautiful images unmistakably recall the story of Narcissus in the third book of Ovid's *Metamorphoses* shortly after the story of Tiresias that had figured so prominently in *The Waste Land*.

This particular myth is especially relevant to the stage of civilisation which Benjamin describes. It commends itself to those in a society that cannot see clearly or readily and confidently understand the nature of the external. The origins of this difficulty antedate the Great War. Both the issue and the employment of the Narcissus theme figure prominently in the work of the symbolist poets.[22] Eliot shares their sensitive awareness not only of the inevitable multiplicity of the poet's voice but also of the never ceasing need for hesitation and qualification in the designating of real experience. All the experiences described in *Four Quartets* are in some way questionable as to authenticity. At the last the most important experience realised by the poem is the act of composition itself, the relating, contextualising, discriminating and patterning of the individual experiences. Patterning proves to be the major experience of the poem and the definition of patterns requires another metaphor from music and from the quartet form.

A necessary preliminary to a description of these musical patternings is a listing of the experiences which they comprise. For despite all the ambiguity in their presentation, the reader is in no doubt that experiences are alluded to in the poem. Within the complex, ever shifting semantic modes of the work, these specific experiences serve as indispensable reference points.

If the title of the work as a whole alerts us to an abstract, involved and highly organised system of expression, the titles of the four individual poems refer to something much simpler and more concrete, four places that are specific, geographically identifiable (in one case by the poet himself) and to some extent physically and topographically described. However great the complexity of each of the quartets, it is possible to say, as a simple initial assumption, that each poem is about a place and about something that happened there. The first section of each quartet evokes the place and the experience with which it is associated. Certain quartets report more than one experience. In the work as a whole there are eight. The various relations subsisting among them and the ways in which they affect and contextualise each other is one of the chief musical features of the poem.

The experiences are not presented in a uniform fashion. Some are rendered very explicitly and circumstantially, others more mutedly. The first section of 'East Coker' contains an experience of the former type:

> Now the light falls
> Across the open field, leaving the deep lane

70

Shuttered with branches, dark in the afternoon,
Where you lean against a bank while a van passes,
And the deep lane insists on the direction
Into the village, in the electric heat
Hypnotised. In a warm haze the sultry light
Is absorbed, not refracted, by grey stone.
The dahlias sleep in the empty silence.
Wait for the early owl.

The experience presented here of walking into a country
village is a simple and familiar one. Both the place and the
mood which it evokes are made very vivid. The use of the
present tense, the stress on the 'now', the use of detail (leaning
against a bank while a van passes) and the strong, pervasive
sense of the soporific warmth of a late summer afternoon all
combine to create a convincing impression of an actuality.

Similar claims might also be made for the descriptions of
experience to be found in the first section of 'Burnt Norton'
and the first section of 'Little Gidding'. Yet not all the
experiences which the poem treats are so fully articulated. In
'Dry Salvages', for instance, the particular experience associated
with this place and informing the poem is much less conspicuous. It is there in the two brief lines:

The salt is on the briar rose,
The fog is in the fir trees.

Cited in isolation these lines appear at most a note, a brief
description of nature and weather. But in their context in the
poem their effect is far more powerful. They occur suddenly

and abruptly between two strongly auditory passages describing and musing on the sounds and movement of the sea. The lineation of the sentence I have quoted and its unexpected visual and tactile quality set it apart from its surroundings. It has something of the character of an imagist poem and is very much an intrusion into the poet's train of speculation and meditation. It gives the impression of being a fragment of an important and assertive memory. The particularised texture that is conveyed in the first line and the chill bleakness there in the second suggest an experience of which even the background details are not to be forgotten. This experience that is suddenly present to the poet's mind is only partially evoked and its autobiographical significance is not made available. Nevertheless, its influence and force within the poem is clear enough. Its very intrusiveness suggests its powerful claims upon the poet's mind. And in a passage describing the sea, within a poem that is concerned with the agony and loss attending on man's ancient struggle with the sea, (concern with death by water recurs in *Four Quartets* and in other poems of Eliot), the two lines may be understood to constitute a richly textured, if brief and understated allusion to an experience of this kind. The very mutedness of the experience that is the initial subject of 'Dry Salvages' is one explanation for the authenticity of the sense of agony which pervades the poem. What we have here is an instance of that power of Eliot which F. R. Leavis in his essay 'Why *Four Quartets* Matters' defines as 'the power of giving concrete definition to (that is, of seizing and evoking in words and rhythms) feelings and apprehensions—the focal core with the elusive aura—that have seemed to him peculiarly significant events in his most private experience.'[23]

There remains one other mode of representing experience in the poem. That is the one in which the poet actually fails to convey the experience adequately and acknowledges his failure. I refer to the opening of the second section of 'East Coker' which begins with the lines, 'What is the late November doing/With the disturbance of the spring'. The experience alluded to in these lines is plainly a crucial one. It completely undercuts the confidently world weary and slightly condescending view of human life derived from, or at least confirmed by, the experiences at the village of East Coker described in the first section of this quartet. And it dominates the remainder of this poem. Yet the passage offers hardly any inkling of the nature of the experience. We are given a sense of violent upset in nature and in the cosmos but that is all. Critics have suggested that the passage might allude to Heraclitus' war of the elements or to Eliot's shock at the onset of the Second World War. Yet these are merely possible associations that the passage may carry with it rather than its intrinsic and contextual import. The feeling evoked by these correlations remains finally too unspecified to be fully intelligible. Perhaps this is the reason for the poet's immediate repudiation of the passage:

> That was a way of putting it—not very satisfactory:
> A periphrastic study in a worn-out poetical fashion,
> Leaving one still with the intolerable wrestle
> With words and meanings.

Manifestly there was an 'it' which the poet sought but failed to describe. He achieved merely a periphrasis rather than an accurate and telling representation. A few lines later on he returns to his endeavour to describe the 'it'. This time his language is much simpler and more modest:

It was not (to start again) what one had expected.
What was to be the value of the long looked forward to,
Long hoped for calm, the autumnal serenity
And the wisdom of age?

This suddenly conversational and less elevated style is itself a possible clue to the experience. Its tone suggests the attitude of humility which the remainder of this passage goes on to consider. The world view, the feeling for life conveyed in the first section now seems an arrogance that was founded on a confidence that proved to be utterly misplaced, because confounded by the unforeseen and the unexpected. The experience of utter personal humiliation, such as appears to be alluded to obliquely here, is not easily detailed without the danger of self-indulgence or of self-dramatisation. (Perhaps there is some element of this latter in the seventeen line passage.) Certainly much detail would be incompatible with the conventions of chamber music and its particular kind of decorum which are among the more important implications of the titular metaphor of quartet. For certain experiences periphrastic studies may be the only civilised form of expression that is available for performer and audience. *Four Quartets* demonstrates and dramatises (as well as discusses) the struggle to represent and interpret experience by means of an acceptable verbal taste. And if it evokes, as critics generally agree it does, certain profundities of experience, it also alludes quite explicitly to those areas of experience which words at that time are unable to reach.

This then is one of the more immediately discernible musical principles informing *Four Quartets,* a movement in the language used between more finely focused reports of experience and lesser and coarser ones. This movement follows a reasonably clear pattern. In the first and in the final quartet experiences are clearly, precisely and convincingly described, while in 'East Coker' and 'Dry Salvages' which evoke more painful memories, the specification is less vivid and confident. But for the musical principles which the title invites us to recall, this might seem to involve an inconsistency in style and diction. (There have, of course, been those who have made this very complaint about the poem.) Yet in a time when the poet has no established rhetoric to which to refer, the differing, contrasting, yet ultimately patterned ways in which a string quartet approaches and reapproaches experience in search of its proper representation and meaning becomes a serviceable device.

There are several other musical modes of representation in the poem besides that of fluctuating intensity. A prominent one is the pattern of sound and of stillness and silence which the sequence of experiences comprises. *Four Quartets* is rooted in very private experiences in remote and unfamiliar places. (Indeed the places named in the four titles are so local that John Hayward, a friend whom Eliot in a prefatory note to the poem thanks for 'improvement of phrase and construction' judged it necessary in his preface to the French translation to say something of their significance to the poet.) Each of these irreducibly particular places has not only its own associations but also its own mood and its own music.

In the opening section of the first quartet, 'Burnt Norton', Eliot recalls a moment of great happiness that happened in the garden of a country house which we know from Hayward to be situated in the Cotswolds near Chipping Camden. In mundane terms the intense moment appears likely to have occurred during an impromptu game of hide and seek with some children whom Eliot senses to be 'Hidden excitedly,

75

containing laughter' somewhere in the garden. He is also aware of them carefully accompanying him in concealment and

> Moving without pressure, over the dead leaves,
> In the autumn heat, through the vibrant air.

The experience is one of pleasant suspense, of happy involvement and of intense yet inexplicit relationship with others. This is the basic experience in the place but in his depiction of it the poet endows it with a good deal more. As we have seen, the vocabulary of these lines associates the experience with many other literary occasions and with traditional notions and moments of religious and mystical illumination. The sense of momentary transcendence is delicately conveyed by the music of this opening section. The slow stately movement of the long lines itself suggests that the moments reported occur 'quietly, quietly,' that the air is 'vibrant', that there is also 'unheard music'. The image in the final section of the quartet of 'the stillness of the violin, while the note lasts', supplies a very fitting restatement of the sound of that aethereal moment of insight with which the poem begins.

The second quartet, 'East Coker', is the richest in experiences; it contains three. The first movement presents what is, as I have suggested, a reasonably detailed account of a visit to East Coker, the village in Somerset where Eliot's ancestors lived before their emigration to America in the seventeenth century. But the poet's pilgrimage is unrewarding. Here there is none of the exhilaration or heightened consciousness experienced at Burnt Norton. There is no music, only 'empty silence'. The place is somnolent, drugged,

76

acquiescent in the mundane order of things. The experience
in this place confirms the poet's sense of the banal predictability
of the processes of life and time as these are observable in
personal and family history. They compare sadly with the
moment of ecstasy evoked and then celebrated in the previous
quartet. The experience at East Coker helps to illustrate and
justify the deduction made after the experience at Burnt
Norton:

> Sudden in a shaft of sunlight
> Even while the dust moves
> There rises the hidden laughter
> Of children in the foliage
> Quick now, here, now, always—
> Ridiculous the waste sad time
> Stretching before and after.

The second experience reported in this quartet is a vision of
the past. It is a description which borrows some of the archaic
vocabulary and orthography of Sir Thomas Elyot's *The Boke
named the Governour* (1531) in order to evoke the dancing and
ceremony of country people of bygone times. Compared to
the 'unheard music' which was one of the paradoxical conditions of the moment of exaltation in the rose garden at Burnt
Norton, 'the music/ Of the weak pipe and the little drum'
which Eliot imagines hearing at East Coker and also the
generations of country dances to which it is the accompaniment sound coarse, heavy and condemned to a stale, unquickened repetitiousness. The heavy, thudding and ultimately
demoralising monotony is markedly there in the following
lines:

77

The time of the seasons and the constellations
The time of milking and the time of harvest
The time of the coupling of man and woman
And that of beasts. Feet rising and falling.
Eating and drinking. Dung and death.

The two experiences in this first movement complement and reinforce each other. The present actuality and the historical vision each support a bored, condescending, slightly disgusted view of the course of human life and history as intrinsically pointless.

The third and final experience contained in this quartet is recorded at the beginning of the second movement. It is an account of how the attitudes expressed in the preceding movement were utterly shattered by a sudden, violent experience of the unforeseeable in life:

What is the late November doing
With the disturbance of the spring
And creatures of the summer heat,
And snowdrops writhing under feet
And hollyhocks that aim too high
Red into grey and tumble down
Late roses filled with early snow?
Thunder rolled by the rolling stars
Simulates triumphal cars
Deployed in constellated wars
Scorpion fights against the Sun
Until the Sun and Moon go down
Comets weep and Leonids fly
Hunt the heavens and the plains

78

> Whirled in a vortex that shall bring
> The world to that destructive fire
> Which burns before the ice-cap reigns.

As we have seen, the experience is, in the poet's own judgement, not successfully realised here. It is rather a rhetorical evocation of a sudden access of awareness, of perhaps a belated, but not to be denied response to that writhing natural world and to those 'creatures of the summer heat', the very beings which in the previous section the poet had felt able confidently to patronise and dismiss. The sound and music of this section comes as a considerable shock. The long, slow, often rather weary lines of the previous movement are replaced by a series of shorter quicker lines. The seventeen lines comprise only two entences and these run on nervously and anxiously. The first sentence finally breaks from syntax. There is a tumbling succession of uneasy adjectival phrases and the sound of the lines, particularly the consonants confirms a sense of thunderous violence. The quiet confident statements of the first movement are completely abandoned.

This shocking disruption of his notions and the new un-expected sense of a common humanity (the 'we' of the second movement that replaces the 'I' of the first) constitutes a major development in the progress of *Four Quartets*. At this stage in the work it has become clear that there is an element of narrative development in the poem. The places, together with the experiences, moods and music that are associated with them, are arranged, collocated and patterned in such a way as to comprise a progress, an education. The third experience in 'East Coker' gainsays the previous two and the world weary generalisations which they induced are now seen to be invalid. The poet's oversimplification of the nature

of time and its processes derives in part from his excessive
valuation of the moment at Burnt Norton and in part from
his narrow, even obsessive preoccupation with it. This view,
he now deduces, was too restrictive and parochially personal.
He must correct the view expressed at the end of 'Burnt
Norton' and offer a new one that will do justice to mundane
humanity:

> Not the intense moment
> Isolated, with no before and after,
> But a lifetime burning in every moment
> And not the lifetime of one man only
> But of old stones that cannot be deciphered.
> There is a time for the evening under starlight,
> A time for the evening under lamplight
> (The evening with the photograph album).

The experience of agony recalled from Dry Salvages, a
place which is, as Eliot himself notes, 'a small group of rocks,
with a beacon, off the N.E. coast of Cape Ann, Massachusetts'
produces yet a further qualification of this view:

> I have said before
> That the past experience revived in the meaning
> Is not the experience of one life only
> But of many generations—not forgetting
> Something that is probably quite ineffable:
> The backward look behind the assurance
> Of recorded history, the backward half-look
> Over the shoulder, towards the primitive terror.

Now, we come to discover that the moments of agony
(Whether, or not, due to misunderstanding,
Having hoped for the wrong things or dreaded the
                                        wrong things,
Is not in question) are likewise permanent
With such permanence as time has.

The experience which in this quartet is restored to the poet's
mind through a long meditation on suffering is, as we have
seen, only glancingly and most reticently evoked. Yet the
attendant mood, the state of feeling which the experience
entails is very present in the memorable music of this quartet.
Here is a characteristically auditory and musical passage:

                    The sea howl
And the sea yelp, are different voices
Often together heard: the whine in the rigging,
The menace and caress of wave that breaks on water,
The distant rote in the granite teeth,
And the wailing warning from the approaching headland
Are all sea voices, and the heaving groaner
Rounded homewards, and the seagull:
And under the oppression of the silent fog
The tolling bell
Measures time not our time, rung by the unhurried
Ground swell.

The many sounds and auditory references in these lines evoke
the sea in a mood that corresponds with human pain, suffering
and lamentation. In the vocabulary, the alliteration (partic-

81

ularly the sibilants) and the difficult often laboured movement of the lines there is conveyed, chiefly through the ear, the sense of an elemental harshness in life. It is a sense and a sound of experience that contrasts markedly with the primitive dance rhythms in 'East Coker' and with the rumbling, somewhat rhetorical evocation of thunder that suddenly shakes the poet out of his complacency. The particular music of 'Dry Salvages' also contrasts sharply with the sound of the final quartet 'Little Gidding'. Here as in 'Burnt Norton' an important attribute of the experience reported is stillness, a stillness which is defined by circumambient sound.

Little Gidding is a Huntingdonshire village where in the seventeenth century Nicholas Ferrar established an Anglican community that was visited by George Herbert and Charles I. Journeying there in midwinter Eliot sees the landscape strangely and significantly illuminated:

The brief sun flames the ice, on pond and ditches,
In windless cold that is the heart's heat,
Reflecting in a watery mirror
A glare that is blindness in the early afternoon.
. . . . . .
                    Now the hedgerow
Is blanched for an hour with transitory blossom
Of snow, a bloom more sudden
Than that of summer, neither budding nor fading,
Not in the scheme of generation.

In the twenty lines that report the experience of midwinter spring there is not a word that refers to sound or that has any very remarkable auditory quality. What is presented is a state of consciousness that is intent, rapt, and essentially still. The stillness here recalls that at Burnt Norton and is utterly different from the music of lament in 'Dry Salvages' or even the hard sounds that we encounter in 'Little Gidding' itself of London under the Blitz where

> . . . . . the dark dove with the flickering tongue
> Had passed below the horizon of his homing
> While the dead leaves still rattled on like tin
> Over the asphalt where no other sound was.

The stillness which is auditorily as well as conceptually defined is the state of consciousness which the poem proposes as its chief object of commendation. The experience in question is, as Eliot asserts in the closing lines of the work, a matter of a very particular kind of hearing. It involves

> The voice of the hidden waterfall
> And the children in the apple-tree
> Not known, because not looked for
> But heard, half-heard, in the stillness
> Between two waves of the sea.

Four Quartets is a patterning of sounds and of music (and of the experiences from which these derive) that is designed to convey to the reader such an apprehension.

There are other patterings too. The succession of experiences also constitutes a progress from the rich but imperfectly understood moment of joy at Burnt Norton to that more fully tutored happiness at Little Gidding. The progress encounters on the way the misapprehensions, delusions and humiliations at East Coker and the suffering associated with the Dry Salvages.

Another principle is the musicalising of the experiences through antithesis and balance. East Coker, the place of family origin, and Little Gidding, the Anglican shrine, are places of purposeful excursion or pilgrimage, places in which the writer sought or expected something. Between these two there is a clear antithesis in that the first brings a view of history that is demoralising while the latter occasions one that makes for joyous resurgence. The first and third quartets, by contrast, deal with places in which significant experience was not consciously and deliberately sought out but unexpectedly received. Again there is a contrast within this pair. 'Dry Salvages' treats of the agony that is inevitable to man, 'Burnt Norton' records a joy that can occur without his control or volition.

The poet leaves us in no doubt about the primacy of these four places as references for his best interpreting of his experience. Other experiences are certainly alluded to. For instance, there seem to have been other moments similar to the one at Burnt Norton; at one point this latter appears in a list of such occasions:

> Whisper of running streams, and winter lightning.
> The wild thyme unseen and the wild strawberry,
> The laughter in the garden . . . .

And Little Gidding is not the only place where such profoundly educative insights may be had:

> There are other places
> Which also are the world's end, some at the sea jaws,
> Or over a dark lake, in a desert or a city —

Nevertheless, there remains a crucial difference between the
places that are alluded to in this way and those which with
varying degrees of intensity are rendered. For these are placed
in a pattern of relationships that grows ever more semantically
rich and intricately textured. What this patterning conveys
ultimately, and all the more compellingly for conveying it in
experiential and musical rather than in conceptual terms, is
that experience is neither gratuitous nor intelligible only in
terms of a supervening principle of order. The places and
experiences are chosen and assembled because in their musical
interaction they precipitate a feeling of the coherent reality
of human life.

There is, of course, much more to this poem than the
reporting of occurrences. There are passages of an altogether
different kind, passages which many readers have found to
be prosaic, unacceptable, a fault in the poem even. C. K. Stead
in his very trenchant account of *Four Quartets* in *The New
Poetic* has this to say of these other parts of the poem:

> *Four Quartets* alternates between, on the one hand the
> 'first voice' of poetry, the voice of 'The Waste Land', less
> perfect now because directed into a conscious mould; and
> on the other the 'second voice', the voice of the man
> 'addressing an audience' in verse barely distinguishable
> from prose. The poem is the expression of a personality
> so fine, so mature, and so supremely intelligent, that to

85

question the achievement may seem only to quibble. But however wise and admirable the man it displays, the poem remains, in this view, imperfectly achieved, with large portions of abstraction untransmuted into the living matter of poetry.[24]

At first sight the distinction proposed here may seem valid. The poem does seem to alternate between those passages which in C. K. Stead's words show how 'the poet's feeling takes form in expressing the visible world' and 'passages expressing conscious ideas and beliefs'. Yet there is more to the work than such clear cut distinctions allow, more to it than 'an uneasy alliance of discourse and Image'. As we actually read the poem our responses are more variegated than this phrase suggests. As we have seen there are four voices in the poem rather than two. And the lecturer's which is the one at which the objections appear to be levelled is not just a voice of dull, 'unpoetic' prose analysis. It is a voice of considerable range. The employment of such supple prose analysis is also a characteristic symbolist procedure. It is, in fact, one of the symbolists' major innovations. Baudelaire, Rimbaud and Mallarmé all wrote poems in prose, a genre which, as Baudelaire once suggested, constituted not a paradox but a genuine and necessary development of the medium of language. In the dedication of his volume *Petits Poèmes En Prose* Baudelaire wrote:

Who among us has not dreamt, in moments of ambition, of the miracle of a poetic prose, musical without rhythm and without rhyme, supple and staccato enough to adapt to the lyrical stirrings of the soul, the undulations of dreams and the sudden leaps of consciousness?

86

Four Quartets is very much a poem of 'leaps of consciousness' and the several kinds of prose poetry within it show how prose is not merely a matter of voice but also a way of perceiving experience. Eliot's first *poème en prose*, 'Hysteria', had been written many years before *Four Quartets*. But now this mode of language recurs in a more sophisticated form. The prose of the poem is not a failing but an important part of its epistemological method. That the poet should attempt a philosophical definition of the incident at Burnt Norton is no more an inconsistency, a lapse or a fault than that he should attempt to represent experience by writing an imitation of Dante in 'Little Gidding'. Both are conscious, difficult and scrupulous efforts to develop a language that is accurate and appropriate to the occasion. Both are stages in that long, sinuous and difficult process of striving to be fully articulate about intense and troubling experiences which is a chief subject of the poem.

The style is various qualitatively as well as formally. Not all the modes of expression essayed are or are intended to be uniformly successful. The writing ranges from the compelling intensity of the description of midwinter spring in 'Little Gidding', to the shy uncertainty and hesitation at the end of the third section of 'East Coker':

> You say I am repeating
> Something I have said before. I shall say it again.
> Shall I say it again?

and to what Donald Davie has justly called the 'inarticulate ejaculations of reach-me-down phrases'[25] in the latter portion of the second section of 'Dry Salvages'. But it is not to the point to extrapolate such passages and to point to them as faults in the poem. For they subserve a larger enterprise. They remind us that the commitment to articulateness cannot and does not remain at the same level of intensity. It can succumb to weariness, uncertainty, inaccuracy and flaccidity. These are all part of the process. The varying modes and qualities of the language convey a sense of often tormenting emotional and intellectual struggle at the very limits of language. The genuineness and validity of this intense struggle, illustrated as it is by 'unpoetic' writing constitute the larger poetic quality of the work.

If the precise effect of *Four Quartets* is something far more complicated and delicate than a clear cut contrast between poetry and abstraction can suggest, it is also true and important to say that the poem is more than a collage of experiences. In 1932 Eliot published in *The Criterion* an essay containing a very clear and succinct account of sonata. It was written by the periodical's music critic J. B. Trend and the principles it describes are quite similar to the ones we can see operating in *Four Quartets:*

A sonata is like a suite in that it is in several movements; but the movements are fewer (usually four), and not all in the same key, while the first and sometimes the last, is constructed on a curious plan which has the effect of arousing the hearer's expectation and then satisfying it. The first movement of a sonata has a pattern like a pattern on a carpet, a pattern in which the different sections are distinct in appearance and contrast with one another, though finally the pattern comes back again to the place where it started. The sonata movement has two chief melodies or 'subjects' which are stated, contrasted, varied, broken up into short phrases and finally stated again near to the end, so that the movement ends in something like conviction or triumph.[26]

What J. B. Trend says here clearly holds true for each of the first movements in the poem and also describes the general principle informing each quartet as a whole. Later in his essay he develops his terminology in a way that is again relevant to the organisation of *Four Quartets*. The 'Musical Chronicle' in *The Criterion* always campaigned vigorously for the recognition of the achievement of 'the new music'; in his article J. B. Trend seeks to explain some of the developments in subject and design that are involved in modern sonata form:

Formerly, listening to music meant listening for tunes and recognising them when they came back, however changed they might be since they last appeared. It meant realising that the tunes would come back, and knowing when to expect them. In listening to the music of today— especially to the music of Schoenberg, Webern, Berg, Hauer and others of the most advanced group—we have to fix our attention not on a melody, but on a melody type, a family of notes in a particular order, something that we remember not as a tune but as a 'mental effect'. We are beginning, in fact, to listen to music in a way which, for over a thousand years, has been Oriental rather than European.[27]

The distinction drawn here between melody and 'mental

effect' helps to explain the disjunction between the musicalised experiences of *Four Quartets,* the passages which are generally recognised as being traditionally poetic, and the remainder of the poem which finds acceptance less easily. Each of the non-experiential passages is an effect of one of the central experiences treated in a quartet. The dichotomy that is of the very nature of sonata is in *Four Quartets* a matter of reverberating interaction of experience and effect. 'Burnt Norton' supplies a clear example. The chief subject of the first part is the important experience in the rose garden. The first part of the second section expresses its most immediate effect, a joyous celebration of the experience and of the feeling about the world which the experience implies. There then follows in the latter part of this section an effect that is less immediate, more removed from the experience in time and more abstract. It is an attempt to capture and to define the experience in philosophical categories. The last eight lines of the section imply a breakdown in this endeavour. They generalise about the experience in less specialised, more everyday language. Here the writing has become slower, less intense, more resigned to the failure to achieve a definitive formulation of the experience and its meaning. Within just one section of the poem we perceive three distinct, successive effects of experience on consciousness. They are not all richly poetic any more than the effects of the modernist music, which J. B. Trend was seeking to explain, are melodic. But as with the 'effects' of which he spoke, Eliot's different modes do record the different ways in which the human mind uses language to make a coherence of experience. J. W. N. Sullivan gives a clear account of the origins and general applicability of sonata pattern:

The four movement sonata form corresponds to a very fundamental and general psychological process, which is the reason why it is found so satisfactory and has been so often employed. The general scheme of a first movement, usually representing a conflict of some kind, followed by a meditative or consoling slow movement, and that by a section easing the way to a vigorous final statement, to the conclusion won, is in its main lines, admirably adapted to exhibit an important and recurrent psychological process. The life-histories of many major psychological processes can be accommodated within this framework.[28]

It would be possible to go through the whole poem tracing the pattern of effects created by the other experiences. But it is more important, in order to do justice to the complex music of Eliot's poem, to consider the more subtle interactions that occur within this principal dialectic. The basic terminology that I have employed must be allowed to be a little more flexible. I have been concerned to talk about the experiences reported in the poem because this seems to me to be a necessary emphasis. But it must be admitted that in certain places in the poem a particular experience can only with difficulty be completely disentangled from its effects. The initial experience at Little Gidding, for example, intense and convincing though it is, emerges gradually from what begins in style and tone as the lecturer's impersonal account of the phenomenon 'midwinter spring'. That is to say that one effect of the experience, the ability to describe it, precedes the experience itself. The occurrences, however vividly actualised in the 'now' are in fact items of memory and, like their effects, are elements in the various assimilative processes of the mind and of memory.

In 'Burnt Norton' also, what we have identified as the major experience of the poem is, in fact, preceded by a long meditation on the nature of time. One might almost say that the recollection of the rose garden is the effect of the experience of thinking about time. The feasibility of this paradox should be recognised if only because it does justice to the intricacies of the poem's sonata form and to the complexities of consciousness which this form so convincingly represents.

With such amended definitions it is possible to say more about the way in which, within the pattern of experiences, the sonata principle persists. For certain experiences turn out to be, at least in part, the effects of other experiences. I have as yet considered only six of the eight experiences, three in 'East Coker' and one in each of the other poems. There remain two more, one in 'Burnt Norton' and one in 'Little Gidding'. I have in mind the experience of being in London. It is vividly presented in the first and third quartets and alluded to again faintly but audibly in the two middle ones. The urban experiences in the work are presented chiefly in the prose of the lecturer. (Interestingly Baudelaire's ideal of the prose poem was very much a product of city life. He envisaged it as a way of being accurate about the complex interactions of urban experience. 'This obsessive ideal', he wrote, 'is above all a child of the experience of great cities, of the intersecting of their myriad relations'. [29]) Eliot's evocations of metropolitan life in each quartet serve to endow the country places named in the four titles with a pastoral significance. The establishment, complication and ultimate reconciliation of this division between an urban and a pastoral consciousness is the sonata pattern which is the chief unifying principle of *Four Quartets* as a whole.

The division is presented very clearly at the outset in 'Burnt Norton'. The description of London here is an antithesis to the description of the manor house garden in Gloucestershire. Whereas in that country place there was a moment of fresh apprehension, excitement, happiness and expectation, in London there are only the predictable and boring processes of the commuter's routine and a soiled and demoralising townscape:

Men and bits of paper, whirled by the cold wind
That blows before and after time,
Wind in and out of unwholesome lungs
Time before and time after.
Eructation of unhealthy souls
Into the faded air, the torpid
Driven on the wind that sweeps the gloomy hills of London,
Hampstead and Clerkenwell, Campden and Putney,
Highgate, Primrose and Ludgate.

This is the same contrast that is referred to in the two important adverbs 'here' and 'there'. London is the here, ('Here is a place of disaffection') and Burnt Norton the there ('I can only say *there* we have been'). These two adverbs will resonate throughout the succeeding poems and with an incremental significance. They also enter into pattern with two other adverbs that similarly recur, 'then' and 'now'. Alluded to in these ways the places come to have far more than a literal meaning. London, the here and now, becomes a state of mind, a state of tired cerebration and speculation, Burnt Norton a richer fuller state of being. The there and the then is invoked to assist in the difficult, often sterile meditations of the here and now.

In 'East Coker' the contrast is continued though in a way

that is not as central to the structure of the quartet. In a poem that radically questions the function of opinion and thought, ('you are not ready for thought') London is the place of an obsessive intellectual activity, which like its many other activities is a futility, an escape from reality. This is seen

> ......when an underground train, in the tube, stops too
>   long between stations
> And the conversation rises and slowly fades into silence
> And you see behind every face the mental emptiness
>   deepen
> Leaving only the growing terror of nothing to think about.

The chief pastoral contrast in this second quartet is between the country dance at the village of East Coker and the dull procession of metropolitan dignitaries. The list reads like a parody of the social page in a newspaper:

> The captains, merchant bankers, eminent men of letters,
> The generous patrons of art, the statesmen and the rulers,
> Distinguished civil servants, chairmen of many committees,
> Industrial lords and petty contractors, all go into the dark,
> And dark the Sun and Moon, and the Almanach de Gotha
> And the Stock Exchange Gazette, the Directory of
>   Directors,
> And cold the sense and lost the motive of action.

In 'Dry Salvages', just as the basic experience itself is only obliquely rendered, so also is the pastoral division. There is conveyed no very vivid sense of actually being in London as there is in all the other quartets. Nevertheless, the reader is kept mindful of the urban perspective and of its inadequacy and superficiality by the mentioning of the obliviousness of 'dwellers in cities' to the realities of life, their commitment to dailiness and to journalism and to the debased forms of prophecy that are

> Pastimes and drugs, and features of the press:
> And always will be, some of them especially
> When there is distress of nations and perplexity
> Whether on the shores of Asia, or in the Edgware Road.

The continuing contrast of here and there comes to a striking finale in 'Little Gidding'. 'East Coker' had reconsidered the meaning of here and there as established in 'Burnt Norton'. In the second quartet the poet concludes that pastoral memories and excursions do not of themselves resolve the difficulties of the 'here'. The 'there' which is East Coker and which was deliberately and hopefully visited brings no new sense of being, though it does have the effect of leading the poet to consider his consciousness in a larger context than in the previous quartet. The journey to his origins was a disappointment of his expectations. But this kind of hope and expectation, it turns out, were misplaced. The injunction now is to 'wait without hope' for 'Here and there does not matter'.

In 'Dry Salvages' this bifurcation is subsumed in a metaphysical and theological antinomy. The intense glimpse of agony recalled from there is related to a much vaster notion of pain and suffering that is shown and felt to be an abiding principle. The only release from or alternative to such a 'there'

95

is a here that is understood conceptually and metaphorically rather than literally. The word here, in fact, is made to relate to the idea of Incarnation:

> Here the impossible union
> Of spheres of existence is actual,
> Here the past and future
> Are conquered, and reconciled.

The capitalisation of the word in these lines is not fortuitous. It is a way of pointing to the new and added significance of the adverb. A few lines later on, it recurs in the lower case:

> For most of us, this is the aim
> Never here to be realised.

The first of several very arresting features of 'Little Gidding' is that this larger, indeed ultimate sense of pastoral is, at least partially, imaged in the here and now. This is what is presented in the opening section. Little Gidding as an experience is an intimation of the truth of the concept described in the previous poem. Also, in this last quartet the clear implication is that Little Gidding is the here and now and London the there. The important urban experience recalled in the second movement is all related in the imperfect tense; the remainder of the poem employs or implies the present tense. The poet who in the previous three quartets wrote from a 'here' that suggested a metropolitan perspective has now, it appears, completed a journey from city to country and from here to there and thus redefined two crucial words. London is at this stage in the poem a 'there', a remembered experience. It is one that is reported to have occurred at the end of a wartime air-raid:

> After the dark dove with the flickering tongue
> > Had passed below the horizon of his homing
> > While the dead leaves still rattled on like tin
> Over the asphalt where no other sound was
> > Between three districts whence the smoke arose
> > I met one walking, loitering and hurried
> As if blown towards me like the metal leaves
> > Before the urban dawn wind unresisting.

The somewhat hallucinatory experience that Eliot has on this occasion, of encountering 'some dead master', some revered mentor in the art of poetry is placed in a musical contrast with the sudden and arresting experience of mid-winter spring at Little Gidding. The latter attests to the actuality, the former to the necessity of some notion of time other than that of simple consecutiveness. In London the dead master discusses poetry and the processes of time. At Little Gidding these urban conceptualisations are experientially validated.

It is noteworthy that the writing in this passage contains none of the disgust that marks the descriptions of London in earlier quartets. The language employed endows the city, the dead master and the wisdom which he has to impart with dignity and significance. The city is here implicitly recognised as a place where people come together. And if the truths which the dead master lists are painful ones, nevertheless the

97

passage reports a valuable (even though hallucinatory) human exchange. The figure of the dead poet is, after all, the only human figure that is at all specified. Contact with him is the first human contact that is reported since the sense of the children in the garden at Burnt Norton. Though the figure is but a vision, his presence both points out and terminates the isolation that informs the consciousness evoked in the poems.

This image of London also constitutes a progress. This urban meeting, the dead master's urbanity and verbal cerebration to which he has devoted his life have a meaning and a value. City as well as country contributes to the final effect of the poem. The 'communication of the dead' in London is a necessary antithesis to that other supra-natural communication which Eliot receives in the Huntingdonshire chapel. Each is in some sense an experience, each an effect. With this final transposition of the here and the there and all that these terms connote, the sonata principle organising the pattern of experiences in the poem comes to its confident and weighty resolution.

Three

Three

The last seventy or so lines of the second part of 'Little Gidding', the passage in which Eliot describes the experience of meeting 'some dead master' in the art of poetry at the end of a bombing attack on London is not only a crucial and culminating item in the economy of *Four Quartets* as a whole but also in the poet's own estimation the most demanding and problematical undertaking in his whole career as a writer. In his comments on this passage in the essay 'What Dante Means To Me' Eliot employs the word 'imitating' as his italicised definition of the particular verbal enterprise that is involved. These lines, he tells us were 'intended to be the nearest equivalent to a canto of the *Inferno* or the *Purgatorio*, in style as well as content that I could achieve'. He then goes on to explain further his purpose and his method:

> The intention, of course, was the same as with my allusions to Dante in *The Waste Land:* to present to the mind of the reader a parallel, by means of contrast between the Inferno and the Purgatorio which Dante visited and a hallucinated scene after an air-raid. But the method is different: here I was debarred from quoting

or adapting at length—I borrowed and adapted freely only a few phrases—because I was imitating.[30]

The technical problems which Eliot encountered in this special kind of poetic undertaking turned out to be in his experience unprecedentedly difficult:

> For one of the interesting things I learnt in trying to imitate Dante in English, was its extreme difficulty. This section of the poem—not the length of one canto of the *Divine Comedy*—cost me far more time and trouble and vexation than any passage of the same length that I have ever written.[31]

In describing these difficult, dense, carefully wrought lines as imitation Eliot associates them with a very specific activity and tradition within the art of poetry. Other instances in English are Pope's *Imitations of Horace,* Johnson's two imitations of Juvenal, 'London' and 'The Vanity of Human Wishes', Fitzgerald's *Rubaiyat of Omar Khayyam* and Pound's *Homage to Sextus Propertius*. Theories of what are involved are similarly long established. Johnson in his *Dictionary* defined imitation as 'A method of translating looser than paraphrase, in which modern examples and illustrations are used for ancient, or domestick for foreign'. Pope in his advertisement to his imitation of Horace's *Ars Poetica* had been more explicit. He tells there how he came to see that some advantage was to be effected by putting Horace into a more modern dress than hitherto he has appeared in, that is, by making him speak, as if he were living and writing now. I therefore resolv'd to alter the Scene from *Rome* to *London,* and to make use of English names of Men, Places, and Customs, where the Parallel would decently permit, which I conceived would give a kind of new air to the Poem, and render it more agreeable to the relish of the present Age . . . . . I have not, I acknowledg, [sic] been over-nice in keeping to the words of the Original, for that were to transgress a Rule therein contained. Nevertheless I have been religiously strict to its sense, and exprest it in as plain and intelligible a manner, as the Subject would bear.

This kind of effort to make a recreation of another poet's work, rather than a word for word translation, to make the other poet speak 'as if he were living and writing now' is a familiar item in classical literary theory. Ben Jonson in his *Timber* lists such an ability as one of the indispensable skills of the poet: 'The third requisite in our *Poet,* or Maker, is Imitation, to be able to convert the substance or riches of another Poet, to his own use. To make choise of one excellent man above the rest, and so to follow him, till he grow very Hee . . . . .'

Jonson's words are especially helpful for assessing the complex passage of imitation which forms one of the major conclusions of *Four Quartets.* Jonson's phrases suggest that the act of imitation is not merely literary but also moral, philosophical, even perhaps alchemical and certainly psychological. They coincide with our sense that the imitative description of the dawn meeting in London after the air-raid

103

is no mere literary exercise but rather the terminal stage of the psychological and philosophical processes which it has been one purpose of the poem to record. At the same time the achieving of such thematic conclusions involves the poet in completing in a very particular way the pattern of verbal textures which constitute the poem as poem. In this passage of imitation the relation of the identifiable themes and content of the poems to their form, texture and music as a verbal artefact becomes unusually well illuminated and crucial.

In the passage in 'Little Gidding' the lines that recall Jonson's idea of the necessary relation of the imitator to his model, which is 'so to follow him, till he grow very Hee' come immediately after the uncertain recognition of a 'familiar compound ghost'. The narration continues:

> So I assumed a double part, and cried
> And heard another's voice cry: 'What! are *you* here?'
> Although we were not. I was still the same,
> Knowing myself yet being someone other—,

Here as elsewhere in the poem the experience presented is a mixture of reality and unreality. Clearly it is an hallucination; equally clearly it is a matter of a very detailed and convincing physical actuality. It is a complicated perception that conveys a highly problematical psychological situation. Far more accessible initially is the philosophical definition of the incident. For in the last line cited 'Knowing myself yet being someone other' the contrast of the two participles is recognisable as belonging to one of the major patterns of resonance in the poem. The two words being and knowing pervade *Four Quartets* and continue to assume new connotations, new significance and new experiential texture as the poem develops. This especial concern with ontology also marks the poem as a work of its time. Heidegger's *Being and Time* published in 1927 is another work of *l'entre deux guerres* which shows the period's determination to establish certainties and true foundations. To trace Eliot's treatment of this theme helps to clarify the last major experience that is reported in the poem. At the same time it also serves to illuminate the function within the overall, ever varying texture of the poem of the seventy lines of imitation.

In the last lines of the first quartet the value and implications of the experience at Burnt Norton are formulated in clear cut ontological terms. That which happened there occurred, according to the assessment in the concluding lines of the poem, in a state 'Between un-being and being'. The two concepts refer to the vacuousness of the poet's quotidian reality and to the sense of abundant life and fulfilment which is momentarily glimpsed in the rose garden. The perception is a limited one because 'human kind/Cannot bear very much reality'. At the time of the experience the poet is in neither of the two states of being but is aware of both. He is 'Between un-being and being'. The poem reports and considers a dual state of awareness.

The bifurcation is also the chief principle of the quartet as a pattern of words. The thematic antithesis of 'being' and 'un-being' is reproduced and extended by those essentially musical qualities of the writing that are less explicitly referential. The ever changing character of the rhythm throughout this quartet contributes a great deal to what is conveyed by the poem. Un-being is registered initially by the slow, unquickened and finally unproductive process of reflection in the first ten lines. Being, in contrast, is a matter of the gentle rhythmic acceleration that marks the next lines in the movement, the

105

stately measured tread of the words that describe the experience in the garden and the rapturous haste of the first part of the second movement. This alternation is also accompanied by a contrast, far more pronounced here than in any of the other quartets, between the concrete language in which experience is presented and celebrated and the abstract, even technical language in which its meaning is analysed.

Another tension within the language of 'Burnt Norton', as within that of the other quartets, results from the need for unabating struggle in order to maintain syntactical control. The uncertainty of connection between the abstruse subject matter and the capacities of the poet's received verbal medium are nowhere more apparent than in the varying adequacy of the sentence forms. In 'Burnt Norton' neither 'being' nor 'unbeing' proves susceptible to the ordered statements which the poet attempts to achieve. After the experience in the garden the world of un-being becomes a tedious incoherence as the syntactical fragmentation in the description of it makes clear:

> Only a flicker
> Over the strained time-ridden faces
> Distracted from distraction by distraction
> Filled with fancies and empty of meaning
> Tumid apathy with no concentration
> Men and bits of paper, whirled by the cold wind
> That blows before and after time,
> Wind in and out of unwholesome lungs
> Time before and time after.

The world of being also resists syntactical patterning. The

poet's sustained attempt to analyse it fails utterly to sub-ordinate itself to the principles of the sentence. It is merely a sequence of phrases and qualifications that achieves at best a faint echo of eighteenth century antithesis at the end. And this makes the unorthodoxy of the remainder of the sentence all the more apparent:

> The inner freedom from the practical desire,
> The release from action and suffering, release from the
> > inner
> And the outer compulsion, yet surrounded
> By a grace of sense, a white light still and moving,
> *Erhebung* without motion, concentration
> Without elimination, both a new world
> And the old made explicit, understood
> In the completion of its partial ecstasy,
> The resolution of its partial horror.

In a poem in which the choice of words is so careful and so telling the recourse to the German word can only be highly conspicuous. It serves to illuminate further the strain that informs the passage. The tension is semantic as well as syntactical. The poet's verbal resources are here very much at their limit.

The using of language, we realise again, is one of the chief experiences that *Four Quartets* treats. The poem offers a report and evidence, as we see from the last quotation, of the author actually testing the limits of language. The poem attempts a description of the human condition by proceeding from the assumption that man may be defined as a language user. As with the other experiences in the poem the problems of language acts are presented in what the reader accepts as both conscious and unconscious ways. The nine lines that I have just cited show the writer in the very act of contending with the inadequacy of available vocabulary and syntax for what he aspires to say. Some lines in the final movement of the quartet indicate a conscious awareness of the difficulty:

> Words strain,
> Crack and sometimes break, under the burden,
> Under the tension, slip, slide, perish,
> Decay with imprecision, will not stay in place,
> Will not stay still.

The problem of words and of placing them properly may be solved, so the conclusion of 'Burnt Norton' runs, by the principles of form and pattern:

> Only by the form, the pattern,
> Can words or music reach
> The stillness, as a Chinese jar still
> Moves perpetually in its stillness.
> Not the stillness of the violin, while the note lasts,
> Not that only, but the co-existence,
> Or say that the end precedes the beginning,
> And the end and the beginning were always there
> Before the beginning and after the end.

But this theoretical statement itself is, as the stumbling syntax of the second sentence shows, as struggling, as tentative, as

108

little in control as that earlier verbal act which it purports to explain. This secondary verbal consciousness can no more explain with confidence the difficulties of the initial verbal consciousness than that earlier consciousness could itself adequately accommodate experience.

To have to consider every statement in a poem as a verbal experience on the author's part as well as a communication to the auditor or reader is to attend to language far more attentively than is normal in contemporary language culture. Yet this kind of respect for the implication of the word is precisely what *Four Quartets* undertakes and requires. It is a poem about the layers of verbal consciousness. Thus the last lines cited are both a precipitate of earlier verbal experience and a verbal act in themselves from which other such acts will derive. They enunciate a realisation of commitment to an allusive, metaphysical notion of language (the exotic quality of which is suggested by the 'Chinese jar') and a rejection of a mundane belief in words, sentences and referentiality. (Such a rarefied theory of language corresponds with the aethereal experience of being which is presented as the highest state of consciousness achieved in the quartet.) Yet the following quartets will present a widening experience of language which will lead eventually in the last section of 'Little Gidding' to a very considerable emendation of the view of language essayed in 'Burnt Norton'. The initial simple antitheses in thinking about language and being start to undergo correction in the second quartet.

'East Coker' contains no intimation of something beyond the temporal such as is to be found in 'Burnt Norton'. Like 'Dry Salvages' it is confined to urgent examination and analysis of the ordinary processes of time as these are psychologically, familiarly or socially experienced. The language of this second poem contrasts markedly with the dialectical abstractions of

'Burnt Norton' in that it consistently and sometimes shockingly emphasises material and physical processes:

> The dripping blood our only drink,
> The bloody flesh our only food:

>   Feet rising and falling.
> Eating and drinking. Dung and death.

> Old stone to new building, old timber to new fires,
> Old fires to ashes, and ashes to the earth
> Which is already flesh, fur and faeces,
> Bone of man and beast, cornstalk and leaf.

The slow heavy rhythms that recur in 'East Coker' convey the author's weary sense of the futility of these processes. Time and history are here felt to be inferior and also utterly unconducive to being. The old customs and rituals of the country people described by Sir Thomas Elyot bring no more awareness of being than do the rituals of modern men and their governors:

> The captains, merchant bankers, eminent men of letters,
> The generous patrons of art, the statesmen and the rulers,
> Distinguished civil servants, chairmen of many
>   committees,
> Industrial lords and petty contractors . . . . .

The slow quickly predictable rhythm of this procession establishes the lifelessness of standard modern rituals. All the titles, social descriptions and honorifics constitute a dead language for in no way do they subserve any genuinely vital purpose. Appropriately enough the familiar gang of phrases concludes at a funeral. But this in turn also proves to be an unreal ceremony:

And we all go with them, into the silent funeral,
Nobody's funeral, for there is no one to bury.

The complexity and imperfect clarity of the pronoun references in this important sentence are very reminiscent of a passage in Heidegger's *Being and Time*. The 'they' of everyday life, of what Heidegger calls Dasein is, he argues, a pronominal device for the avoidance of responsibility and 'being':

The 'they' is there alongside everywhere [ist überall dabei], but in such a manner that it has always stolen away whenever Dasein presses for a decision . . . . . It can be answerable for everything most easily, because it is not someone who needs to vouch for anything. It 'was' always the 'they' who did it, and yet it can be said that it has been 'no one'. In Dasein's everydayness the agency through which most things come about is one of which we must say that 'it was no one'.[32]

Heidegger's view of the furtive inauthenticity of social processes and of the individuals who as 'they' constitute them

111

is not the only parallel with Eliot's poem. Another shared realisation is that everyday existence (Dasein) can obscure, reduce and destroy more important states of consciousness. A few lines earlier Heidegger writes:

Thus the 'they' maintains itself factically in the averageness of that which belongs to it.....it keeps watch over everything exceptional that thrusts itself to the fore. Every kind of priority gets noiselessly suppressed. Overnight, everything that is primordial gets glossed over as something that has long been well known . . . . . This care of averageness reveals in turn an essential tendency of Dasein which we call the 'levelling down' [Einebnung] of all possibilities of Being.

Similarly 'East Coker' recognises that the mundane processes of time and of language can damage the remembrance and the interpretation of an experience such as that recorded in 'Burnt Norton'. The clear cut antithetical notions of time and of being established in the earlier quartet are here utterly confounded. The unproblematical idea of un-being as 'the waste sad time/Stretching before and after' is completely and humiliatingly invalidated by the experience reported in the second movement. Time as it is known to human beings may not be patterned and understood in this patronising way:

For the pattern is new in every moment
And every moment is a new and shocking
Valuation of all we have been . . . .

112

The first word of the phrase 'all we have been' plainly implies that the greatly prized experience at Burnt Norton must also be reassessed in terms of this new more complex understanding of time. But the revaluation brings a reduction in the intensity of the memory. Throughout the first half of the poem there is a sense of loss. (The poem later becomes, quite explicitly, a 'fight to recover what has been lost'.) And as the author becomes more and more caught up in the difficult processes of mundane time, he has to acknowledge his involvement, his identification with the 'we all' who are carried along into un-being. 'And we all go with them into the silent funeral'. The poet now finds himself in that state so much reported by modern literature in which he feels his own best nature and awareness to be compromised, falsified and reduced.

What follows is thematically and in verbal texture a crucial passage in 'East Coker'. With a striking change of tense that suggests the poet's prior consciousness of (and thus dissociation from) this destructive continuum, three ostentatious, virtuoso metaphors are introduced to describe the determined act of will by which such release was effected. Paradoxically the stillness which is proposed as freedom from the futile motions of contemporary society is imaged by occasions that are particular to that society. The sudden darkening of the stage in the theatre, the silence in the underground train, the state of consciousness induced by the administration of ether all belong to that urban mode of existence which elsewhere in the poem has been presented as 'un-being'. Urban society, it turns out, contains metaphors for freedom. The simple pastoral dialectic has been redefined.

'East Coker' proves to be a discrimination of rituals. Its chief principle of organisation is the dual meaning of the word ritual in present English. Pejoratively the word denotes a pointless routine: originally it meant the performance of a

113

set of pre-ordained acts for the achievement of a particular end. The writing in the poem gives evidence of both meanings of the word. The chief endeavour of the poem is to identify dead verbal rituals such as that at the funeral and to realise new rituals, new and performable acts that may publicly witness, steward and conserve 'being'. The poem tries to find new verbal rituals to take the place of the dead ones.[33] As is likely to be the case with anyone who undertakes to offer such forms of ontological genuineness the poet is often nervous and uncertain, even perhaps embarrassing in his enterprise. The fourth movement of the quartet, for instance, which attempts the ritual language of the hymn is marked by a certain emotional imbalance. The rather crude fundamentalist symbolism in the first two stanzas and the physical distaste and coarse irony of the last two have the stridency of a desperate and necessarily unpolished effort to supply a statement for personal and for collective reassurance. The panicky return to the first person singular in the penultimate stanza, the failure to sustain the 'we' of earlier verses also illustrates the difficulties involved in sustaining this ritual statement.

Ritual as it characterises the linguistic texture of 'East Coker' is essentially a matter of establishing an association with other people. It entails a critique of the solipsism of 'Burnt Norton' and the search for a form of human solidarity that will serve to counteract the depredations of time and to make formal, public recognition of realities that offer freedom from time. The language of this second quartet is more socialised than that of the first. The conclusions about language and poetry in the second and fifth movements are, as we have seen, offered chiefly in the voice of the conversationalist. Discussion becomes recognised as a necessary ritual:

114

So here I am, in the middle way, having had twenty
                                        years—
Twenty years largely wasted, the years of *l'entre*
                                        deux guerres
Trying to learn to use words . . . . .

There is the further recognition that the use of language, the
writing of poetry and the ontological quest must be co-
operative acts:

                              And what there is to
        conquer
By strength and submission, has already been discovered
Once or twice, or several times, by men whom one cannot
        hope
To emulate—but there is no competition—
There is only the fight to recover what has been lost
And found and lost again and again: and now, under
        conditions
That seem unpropitious . . . .

The chief ontological conclusions of this quartet are also
expressed in a language of ritual. After some tonal uncertainty
the final passage of the third movement attempts the sermon
form. The new awareness of knowing and being is very plainly
a derivative from the experiences of this poem:

    In order to possess what you do not possess
        You must go by the way of dispossession.

115

In order to arrive at what you are not
    You must go through the way in which you are not.
And what you do not know is the only thing you know
And what you own is what you do not own
And where you are is where you are not.

The initial hesitations and the element of mystification in these lines are a reminder that such a passage is again but a stage in the development of an understanding. Essentially the same point will be made in more homely words in the concluding lines of this quartet. And the notion of a proper and careful approach to the understanding of temporal existence as a condition of being will be resumed and radically developed in the next quartet, 'Dry Salvages'.

A unique feature of this third poem is that it achieves no explicit conclusion concerning the nature of language and poetry. One possible explanation of this and one that would support those who find serious deficiencies in the quality of the writing in 'Dry Salvages' is that there is here a tacit recognition on the poet's part of a failure of verbal and poetic realisation. But it is surely more than an index of poetic inadequacy. (It is part of the poet's method, as we have seen in 'East Coker' to acknowledge and to discuss instances of failure.) It seems more likely to be a clue to the incapacity of available language for fully identifying and accommodating the particular issues of experience which the poem approaches. Here as elsewhere in *Four Quartets* the writing gives a sense of what can only be termed the limits of the powers of language.

The quartet begins by proceeding with the task, the necessity of which was realised at the end of 'East Coker' of exploring further into the nature of man's temporal condition. Human consciousness, which in the second quartet had been experienced as something painfully susceptible to the deceptions of time, is in the opening lines of 'Dry Salvages' shown to be similarly vulnerable to the unpredictable workings of its own unconscious, here metaphorised as the river. The easy expansiveness of the writing here suggests that this is not a genuine act of exploration, no authentic lived struggle to realise the borders of human consciousness. Given what follows, these lines come to seem part of the facile, comfortably circumscribed, psycho-analytical notion of consciousness which by the end of the poem will be explicitly dismissed. The poet writes that to

> dissect
> The recurrent image into pre-conscious terrors—
> To explore the womb, or tomb, or dreams; all these are
>   usual
> Pastimes and drugs, and features of the press.

The journalese editorialising style of the first ten lines of 'Dry Salvages' are as insufficient linguistically as the notion of consciousness which they define. *Four Quartets* assumes the language of psychology to be easier and less revealing of human realities than the language of ontology.

'Dry Salvages' then modulates into a passage that introduces another metaphor for a further specification of the human condition. The lines envision human consciousness as something reaching back over vast extents of ancient and indeed pre-historic time:

> The tolling bell
> Measures time not our time, rung by the unhurried

117

Ground swell, a time
Older than the time of chronometers.

One condition of such tracts of evolutionary time as the poem imagines them, is suffering. This is one of the rare permanencies of time. The rivers of the individual temperament and the ancient oceans of history have their own mutations, but suffering metaphorised as the submerged, menacing rock has persistent, unchanging being. The verbs in the concluding lines of the second movement reiterate and insist upon this new realisation of suffering as a perpetual component of being:

On a halcyon day it is merely a monument,
In navigable weather it is always a seamark
To lay a course by: but in the sombre season
Or the sudden fury, is what it always was.

The difficulty of confronting suffering through the medium of what in 'Little Gidding' will be explicitly alluded to as 'this year's language' is the main theme of this third quartet. The lack of public style for talking accurately and creatively about suffering is one of the plain inferences of the poem. In attempting to go beyond the verbal habits of the press and popular psychology the poem achieves only a strained, insistent discursiveness which sets it apart from the other three quartets. This I take to be the chief reason for the singular absence of any new insight into the nature of poetic language in this poem.

But along with this implied recognition of such failure there goes an effort to imagine ways in which it might be overcome. The references to Krishna are important instances of this. Though the poet cannot easily accommodate the fact of agony in his own words in his own time, he can in borrowed words envision and invoke such an essentially prophetic style:

> While time is withdrawn, consider the future
> And the past with an equal mind.
> At the moment which is not of action or inaction
> You can receive this: 'on whatever sphere of being
> The mind of a man may be intent
> At the time of death'—that is the one action
> (And the time of death is every moment)
> Which shall fructify in the lives of others:
> And do not think of the fruit of action.

The three lines from Krishna about being occur within a section (not all of which is quoted here) which is itself a borrowing. It is a translation not from another language but from another medium, that of music. The prophetic voice which Eliot is able to imagine speaking to passengers on an ocean crossing who are suspended from their ordinary routines is a voice which does not employ words. It is musical rather than verbal:

> At nightfall, in the rigging and the aerial,
> Is a voice descanting (though not to the ear,
> The murmuring shell of time, and not in any language).

The various failures of language in 'Dry Salvages' now become

119

more fully explained. That further realisation of being which acknowledges and contains agony cannot be evoked in ordinary language. Language may at best offer a transcription. These last lines of the third quartet confront the very same need and the same difficulty which Mallarmé describes in one of his essays. He is wondering about the motives of the audience at a concert:

> This great audience fulfilled by the trivial game of existence as this is elevated into politics and described day after day by the press; how is it, (it is based on an instinct to go beyond the intervals of the literary?) that this audience suddenly needs to be face to face with the Unsayable or the Pure, poetry without words?[34]

'Dry Salvages' perpetuates this symbolist tradition of regarding being as something musical. The most creative use of language is to surpass the medium of language and to assume the powers of another medium, music. In 'Dry Salvages' as in 'Burnt Norton' full consciousness is defined as a musical condition. And the last few lines of this third quartet complicate the notion of music even further. They speak of a

> music heard so deeply
> That it is not heard at all, but you are the music
> While the music lasts.

The related concepts of language as music and of music as something which is truly unheard are both hallmarks of symbolism and of the metaphysical tradition from which it derives. 'Mallarmé, who could have subscribed to Plato's aphorism, repeated by Pater that "all art aspires to music", rediscovers for himself the Platonic and Pythagorean conception that the universe is musically constructed, and the human soul, which is similarly formed, cannot hear through the sensorial apparatus of the body the celestial music of its source. Therefore heard music is inferior to unheard music which is the true wisdom of Plato . . . . .'[35]

These notions will serve chiefly to illuminate the particular verbal method of *Four Quartets*. It is musical in that its patterns of feelings, moods and poetic successes and failures constitute a communication that is other than a sequence of discourse. Also in what is said there is predicated something that is unsaid. The unheard music proves to be a valid analogy for the method of the poem. The conditions of existence are presented in such a way that the human desire for understanding and for principles of containment and unification is also there, if not explicitly, then by pattern and by inference.

Other implications for Eliot's chamber music of the essentially symbolist statement 'you are the music/While the music lasts' are pursued in 'Little Gidding'. The concern with individual consciousness and being, with the deeper meanings of the two words 'you are' comes to what is very much an experiential resolution in this final quartet. And for a poetic sequence which gives such a strong sense of inner voices and only a tentative sense of involvement with present actuality, the denial of isolation and solipsism is strikingly emphatic and unambiguous. The unmistakeable inference of 'Little Gidding' is that the individual consciousness is not and cannot be hermetic. The pattern of experiences which it presents refutes the idea that was broached earlier of the inevitability of atomistic and inauthentic existence.

121

'Little Gidding' takes up certain hints about the nature of the self contained in earlier quartets. In 'East Coker' the folly of the old men is pre-eminently their cultivation of hermetic selfhood, 'their fear of possession,/Of belonging to another, or to others or to God'. And in 'Dry Salvages' the highest available activity for man is described as 'Ardour and selflessness and self-surrender'. Such insights prepare the way for the important moment of experience after the air raid on London. The moment is a crisis for the poet's selfhood as it is for his city and his civilisation. The nature of this development is summarised in the half dozen words in which he describes himself 'Knowing myself yet being someone other'. Such consciousness is very familiar, even particular to the major literature of this century. The antithesis is as central to Yeats's later poems and to *Ulysses* as it is to *Four Quartets* and can be seen to result from a stage in civilisation in which rapid accretions in definitions of consciousness threaten to obscure and deny its deeper origins. D. H. Lawrence, whose chief novels also focus upon the workings of the dialectic of being and knowing, once offered this definition of the antithesis:

So, facing both ways, like Janus, face forward, in the quivering, glimmering fringe of the unresolved, facing the unknown, and looking backwards over the vast rolling tract of life which follows and represents the initial movement, man is given up to his dual business of being, in blindness and wonder and pure godliness, the living stuff of life itself, unrevealed; and of knowing with unwearying labour and unceasing success, the manner of that which has been, which is revealed.[36]

For all the great distance that there is between Lawrence's philosophical assumptions and Eliot's and for all the difference in their ways of sensuously apprehending and representing the world, this passage serves admirably as a summary of the sort of awareness that is achieved in the second movement of 'Little Gidding'. What this poem offers as conclusion to the sequence is a balancing of the delicate, ephemeral, very un-Lawrencean sense of being imaged as 'midwinter spring' and the knowledge which the 'dead master' has to impart. The two experiences reported in this quartet interact and complement each other. Being is not a mindless mystification; knowing is now experientially grounded. The unity, the reconciliation which 'Little Gidding' conveys is a synthesis of the two experiences.

This final state stands in marked contrast to the greatly cherished moment of very private consciousness at Burnt Norton. By the end of the sequence he has moved beyond the parochialism of the self. He now regards the self as something variously involved with other people and with other modes of being. The insight is represented by the compound figure of the dead master who is himself not 'one but many'. He is an instance and an amalgam of the many poets who have renewed and transmitted the language that Eliot now uses. He illustrates the presence of the dead in the phenomenon of language and poetry. Man defined as language user is, as Mallarmé so often suggests in his Tombeau poems, manifestly involved in extra-personal realities.

In allowing his voice to be used by the visitant, in acquiescing in this necessary subordination, the poet makes conscious recognition of this fact of existence. He and his consciousness become, like language itself, not an absolute but a medium. The actual and practical living out of this recognition entails the act of imitation as this has been defined earlier. It is the

123

way in which the poet achieves release from that hermetic egotism which is a recurrent assumption in symbolist poetry and of which Mallarmé's *Hérodiade* is the pre-eminent example. The final achievement of *Four Quartets* is the winning of a language that conveys the larger contexts of the self and even causes the very category of the self to become redundant:

See, now they vanish,
The faces and places, with the self which, as it could,
    loved them,
To become renewed, transfigured, in another pattern.

The long and memorable passage of imitation which constitutes the centrepiece of the final quartet also illuminates another filament in the verbal texture of the sequence, the pattern of direct quotation. The poet is much more frugal in his use of quotation in *Four Quartets* than in *The Waste Land*. In that earlier poem, the consciousness of the speaker, Tiresias, is for the most part a collage of quotations from the past. The literary fragments reveal a mind that can neither impinge on the present nor, as a result of this failure, make a living coherence of the past. Though concerned with such solipsism, the conclusion of *Four Quartets* is distinctly different. The voices which we hear in this last major poem, for all their testing of realities and for all the ambiguities and uncertainties in the relation of performers of chamber music to audience, do not speak only of the futility of language or confuse themselves by choosing verbal fragments to shore against ruins. There is here an awareness similar to that which Wagner discovered in Beethoven's late quartets. Interestingly Wagner saw the Beethoven of these works as a Tiresias figure,

124

but one that is significantly different from that of *The Waste Land*. In these last quartets, he maintains, Beethoven, like Tiresias, who was barred from the world of things seen and to whom it was granted instead to perceive the reason for all things with his inner eye, is 'the deaf musician who listens to his inner harmonies undisturbed by the noise of life, who speaks from the depths to a world that has nothing more to say to him'.[37] Eliot's *Four Quartets* report both a similar isolation and a similarly intransigent denial of solipsism. The past is more than the sterile remains of an individual, it is part of a living continuum. In *Four Quartets* the use of quotation amounts to more than the making of a literary museum. It is one of the ways in which the past assists at the understanding of the present. It serves to support the pattern and the development of the poem. The first quartet contains no direct quotation; it is wholly private and personal in its concerns. The second cites and then comes to value Sir Thomas Elyot's description of necessary rituals. The third cites Krishna as a way of establishing the notion of modes of being. And 'Little Gidding' quotes from Dame Julian of Norwich and *The Cloud of Unknowing* as a way of wording explicitly the hope and belief that are implied in the collocating of the last two experiences. All the quotations are statements about ontology. They establish the range of theories of being upon which the poem draws.

The quotations also serve to emphasise what is meant by the verbal enterprise of imitation. Quotation and imitation are similar and yet ultimately very different acts. The former is a matter of referring to the past, of alluding to a verbal artefact, an insight or a truth. The latter is a matter of 'being someone other' verbally, an act of empathy, a realisation that, because of language, the self is constituted of other people and of the dead as well as the living. It is to this that

125

Eliot refers in the final movement of 'Little Gidding' where he requires of the language of poetry

> An easy commerce of the old and the new,
> The common word exact without vulgarity,
> The formal word precise but not pedantic,
> The complete consort dancing together.

In these lines the word is regarded as something far more reliable than it had been at the end of 'Burnt Norton'. In the same way that experience in general as it is presented in the poem has taught the poet a new humility and a new wisdom, the specifically linguistic experiences presented in the poem have brought a new understanding of the poet's medium of language. Words are no longer disparaged as the undependable means of attaining a larger end. Words and phrases and sentences may be 'right'. Furthermore words are not subordinated to the poet but rather he to them or rather to that continuum which is their condition:

> For last year's words belong to last year's language
> And next year's words await another voice.

It is the poet's task to arrange this year's words in such a way as to create a language that shall realise and communicate the authentic. The chief characteristic of such language as it is described in the final section of 'Little Gidding' is a unity born of the proper balancing of antithesis. And of this the final quartet is itself an instance. There is here none of the

126

polarisation of language which we find in 'Burnt Norton' and none of the strain and failure of the middle quartets. The act of imitation exemplifies the new dispassionate view both of the self and of the medium. The language of 'Little Gidding' is calm and deliberate throughout. There is a balance in the language just as there is in the patterning of experience. Verbally as well as thematically the end of the ontological quest is a reconciliation of opposites in a higher synthesis.

The realisation of such unity is the purpose and the *raison d'être* of the quartet form. And this is why the form has been traditionally one to which older artists resort. 'The form of composition known as the string quartet must be a work of maturity, if it is to have any real artistic significance.'[38] So writes the nineteenth century critic and theorist Vincent d'Indy in his study of César Franck. He goes on to say that 'the string quartet is the most difficult of all forms to treat worthily and that in order to attain the variety in unity which it essentially demands, ripeness of intellect and talent, together with sureness of touch are indispensable qualities'.[39] *Four Quartets* is very much a work of this kind of maturity. The first quartet was published in the poet's forty-eighth year and the last one in his fifty-fourth. The sequence is a major poet's last attempt to understand and resolve the conflicts in his medium, his art and his experience. That the unity towards which the poem works and moves requires formulation in scrupulously careful ontological terms is a measure of both the intellectual power and the verbal texture and daring of the work. In this way more than in any other the sequence invites and risks comparison with Beethoven's late quartets.

To many readers of the poem Eliot's specifically Christian ontology will be of little interest. Indeed, even that more general concern with the authentic which he shares with

127

Heidegger already appears something that is particular to that period of *l'entre deux guerres* which, as writers such as George Orwell and Walter Benjamin remind us, was especially troubled by the multiplication of falsities, jargon and a sense of unreality. More than thirty years after the completion of the poem the momentous historical context of its composition, like its philosophy, has become removed from the experience of many of its readers. Our concern with the highly wrought verbal texture of the poem leads us to forget that it is a poem of the thirties and the forties, or, almost exactly of the Hitler period. The first quartet was published just a few weeks after the German army moved into the Rhineland in March 1936. And the remaining three appeared during the early years of the Second World War when Nazi victory seemed probable and imminent. 'Little Gidding' deals in great part with the experience of the London air-raids; 'Dry Salvages' takes on a new resonance when we recall that it was written at the height of the war in the Atlantic, that ocean which has a special significance for Eliot and for the *Quartets*.[40] This historical background makes the patriotism and metaphysics of freedom presented in 'Little Gidding' more understandable. It also makes the patient verbal crafting of the poem that much more admirable. The concerns, the moods and ideas of that time recede from us. But the verbal tension, struggle and achievement of the poem still seem very contemporary. More compelling to us than the philosophical assumptions such as the allusions to pre-Socratic ontology (which again Eliot shares with Heidegger) are the acts of language which make up the poem. The final authenticity to which the poem alludes is, admittedly, a theological and a philosophical matter. But its value and distinction as a literary masterpiece lie in its persevering endeavour to authenticate ever more finely the language used, to employ words in such a way as to realise

128

(at the cost of whatever complication) a genuine voice, to designate true experience and to realise the frontiers of expression. These are large enterprises for what we are prone to think of as a limited and modest form. It is one of the several paradoxes of the quartet form employed by Haydn, Mozart, Beethoven and Eliot that it is able to accommodate such a range and such profundities of experience.

Notes

Preface

1. "I mentioned the *Four Quartets*. 'I stand or fall on them,' Eliot stated emphatically." W. T. Levey, *Affectionately, T. S. Eliot* (New York, 1968), p. 120.

Introduction

2. T. S. Eliot, 'From Poe to Valéry' in *To Criticize the Critic* (London, 1965), p. 42.
3. Hugh Kenner, *The Pound Era* (Berkeley and Los Angeles, 1971), p. 133.
4. T. S. Eliot, 'Baudelaire In Our Time' in *Essays Ancient And Modern* (London, 1936), p. 73.
5. Charles Baudelaire, 'Theophile Gautier' in *Selected Writings On Art and Artists,* translated by P. E. Charvet (Harmondsworth, 1972), p. 261.
6. Baudelaire, *op. cit.,* p. 272.
7. As in all subsequent passages from Mallarmé, the English version is my own. Since it is very difficult to reproduce both the subtle, punctilious emphases and the syntactical tortuousness of this prose, I here supply, as in the case of other translations from Mallarmé, the French original.

   A quoi bon la merveille de transposer un fait de nature en sa presque disparition vibratoire selon le jeu de la parole, cependant; si ce n'est pour qu'en émane, sans la gêne d'un proche ou concret rappel, la notion pure.

   Stéphane Mallarmé, *Oeuvres Complètes* (Paris, Pléiade Edition, 1956), p. 368.
8. *ibid.,* pp. 367–368.

   Certainement, je ne m'assieds jamais aux gradins des concerts, sans percevoir parmi l'obscure sublimité telle ébauche de quelqu'un des poëmes immanents à l'humanité ou leur originel état, d'autant plus compréhensible que tu et que pour en déterminer la vaste ligne le compositeur éprouva cette facilité de suspendre jusqu'à la tentation de s'expliquer. Je me figure par un indéracinable sans doute préjugé d'écrivain, que rien ne demeurera sans être proféré; que nous en sommes là, précisément, à rechercher, devant une brisure des grands rythmes littéraires (il en a été question plus haut) et leur éparpillement en frissons articulés proches de l'instrumentation, un art d'achever la transposition, au Livre, de la symphonie ou uniment de reprendre notre bien: car, ce n'est pas de sonorités élementaires par les cuivres, les cordes, les bois, indéniablement mais de l'intellectuelle parole à son apogée que doit avec plénitude et évidence, résulter, en tant que l'ensemble des rapports existant dans tout, la Musique.

9. Philip Barford, *The Keyboard Music of C. P. E. Bach* (London, 1965), p. 83.
10. For an account of this reference to the Beethoven quartets see Grover Smith. *T. S. Eliot's Poetry and Plays* (Chicago, 1956), p. 253. It has also been reported that Eliot had in mind Bartok's Quartets, numbers 2–6. See Hugh Kenner, *The Invisible Poet* (London, 1974), p. 261.
11. J. W. N. Sullivan, *Beethoven His Spiritual Development* (London, 1972), pp. 109–110.
12. Maynard Solomon, 'Beethoven, Sonata and Utopia', *Telos,* 9, Fall 1971, p. 43.
13. Reginald Barrett Ayres, *Joseph Haydn And The String Quartet* (London, 1974), p. 71.
14. A description of such a gathering is to be found in the memoirs of Michael Kelly, the eighteenth century Irish tenor who was the first Don Basilio in Mozart's *Marriage of Figaro.* See Michael Kelly, *Reminiscences* (London, 1826), Vol. 1, pp. 240–241.

One

15. Mallarmé, *op. cit.* p. 370
    L'écrivain, de ses maux, dragons qu'il a choyés, ou d'une allégresse, doit s'instituer, au texte, le spirituel histrion.
16. Robert Langbaum, *The Poetry of Experience: The Dramatic Monologue in Modern Literary Tradition* (New York, 1963), p. 107.

17. See Lionel Trilling, *Sincerity and Authenticity* (London, 1974), pp. 27–28.
18. R. Bowen, ed., *Diderot: Rameau's Nephew and Other Works* (Indianapolis, 1964), pp. 67–68.
19. Raymond Preston, *'Four Quartets' Rehearsed* (London, 1946), pp. 55–56.

Two

20. Walter Benjamin, 'The Storyteller' in *Illuminations* (London, 1970), pp. 83–84.
21. J. W. N. Sullivan, *op. cit.,* p. 80.
22. In 1891, when he was still a follower of Mallarmé, André Gide published 'Le traité du Narcisse' which treats of concerns that are strikingly similar to those in *Four Quartets*. In the same year Paul Valéry wrote the poem 'Narcisse Parle', his first treatment of a subject to which he was to return again in later years.
23. F. R. Leavis, *English Literature In Our Time And The University* (London, 1969), p. 115. The same author has also published an extended and very important assessment of *Four Quartets* in his *The Living Principle: English as a Discipline of Thought,* London, 1975.
24. C. K. Stead, *The New Poetic* (London, 1964), p. 178.
25. Donald Davie, 'T. S. Eliot: The End of an Era' in *T. S. Eliot's Four Quartets: A Casebook* (London, 1969), pp. 156–157.
26. J. B. Trend, 'Music Chronicle' in *The Criterion,* XLV, July 1932, p. 702.
27. *ibid.,* p. 704.
28. J. W. N. Sullivan, *op. cit.,* pp. 112–113.
29. Charles Baudelaire, *Petits Poèmes en Prose (Le Spleen de Paris)* (Paris, Gallimard, 1973), p. 22.

    Quel est celui de nous qui n'a pas, dans ses jours d' ambition, rêvé le miracle d'une prose poétique, musicale sans rythme et sans rime, assez souple et assez heurtée pour s'adapter aux mouvements lyriques de l'âme, aux ondulations de la rêverie, aux soubresauts de la conscience?

C'est surtout de la fréquentation des villes énormes,
c'est du croisement de leurs innombrables rapports que
naît cet idéal obsédant.

Three

30. T. S. Eliot, *To Criticize The Critic* (London, 1965), p. 128.
31. *ibid.*, p. 129.
32. Martin Heidegger, *Being and Time,* trans. John Macquarrie
    and Edward Robinson (New York, 1962), p. 165.
33. Concern with language as process rather than reference system
    has been clearly described in a recent account of structuralism:
    > Yet, inasmuch as the object is no longer a static one,
    > to be studied in an external way, but rather a form of
    > perception, an awareness of the interplay of the same and
    > the other to be developed, the emphasis on signification
    > takes the form of a mystery, the mystery of the incarnation
    > of meaning in language, and as such its study is a kind of
    > meditation. This is what accounts for the hermetic quality
    > of the writers who deal with it. The sense of the esoteric
    > may be understood, in Barthes' sense, precisely as a sign,
    > as a way of signifying ritual and the presence of mystery,
    > of underlining through the very temporal unfolding of the
    > ritual language the sacred quality of the object itself. It
    > is no accident that the style of Lacan suggests that of
    > Mallarmé, that that of Derrida suggests Heidegger, both
    > of whom expressed in the very movement of their periods
    > the essential nature of the text as initiation.

    (Frederic Jameson, *The Prison-House of Language* (Princeton,
    1972), pp. 168–169.)
34. Mallarmé, *op. cit.,* p. 389.
    > Cette multitude satisfaite par le menu jeu de l'existence,
    > agrandi jusqu'à la politique, tel que journellement le
    > désigne la presse; comment se fait-il—est-ce vrai—cela
    > repose-t-il sur un instinct que franchissant les intervalles
    > littéraires, elle ait besoin tout à coup de se trouver face
    > à face avec l'Indicible ou le Pur, la poésie sans les
    > mots!

35. Joseph Chiari, *Symbolism from Poe to Mallarmé: The Growth of a Myth* (London, 1956), pp. 136–137.
36. D. H. Lawrence, 'Study of Thomas Hardy' in *Phoenix* (London, 1936), p. 430. For a discussion of this issue as it is treated in Lawrence's major novels see Keith Alldritt, *The Visual Imagination of D. H. Lawrence* (London, 1971), pp. 78–96.
37. Richard Wagner, *Beethoven,* trans. Edward Dannreuther (London, 1880), p. 54.
38. Vincent d'Indy, *César Franck,* trans. Rosa Newmarch (London, 1965), p. 182.
39. *ibid.,* p. 184.
40. Some three months before this poem was first printed the battleship 'Hood' was sunk with the loss of over one thousand four hundred lives.

Index

138